THE ROOM OF RETURN

Where Days of Memories Through

ALBERT VICENT

 www.trafford.com
North America & international
toll-free: 1 888 232 4444 (USA & Canada)
fax: 812 355 4082

CONTENTS

The Room Of Return

Where Days of Memories Through

Al Vicent

The Room Of Return

Where Days of Memories Through

by

Albert Vicent

His Memoirs

BEEN

A part of now
In.
The past has been
And
Comes when called
Bringing
With it friends
Building-
A crystal bridge
From
Now to then
Of
Memoirs.

MOMENTO NOTES

As the world went its way along with the years, I followed along my way.

I can remember I think back to about when I was maybe 4 years old playing with my brother Clarence he was about 5 years older than I. We always played together we lived in a little house in Peacock Michigan on a small place of ground. It wasn't too small but small as com- pared to some of the farms I see now where I live in California's farming area where some large farm's cover 80 or more acres.

Our little place was only one acre but Father made a house from old railroad crossties that had been removed from the railroad, Some way he got them to his piece of ground and made the little house where I was born and lived for 17 years with my brother, sister, Mother and Father.

Had some very good times in that old house, I'll never forget it. It didn't have the modern conveniences of homes now, because Peacock Michigan at that time did not have electricity no sewage or things like that, it was strictly country.

Folks had outside toilets, hand pumps for water kerosene lamps for lights in the house coal and wood burning stoves that was it.

Everybody lived that way, we were accustomed to that way of living. In our little one room kindergarten to 8th grade school. There were inside restrooms, the girls restroom was on one side of the building left side, boys on the other side, at rear inside of the school. The restrooms had a large water tank at its base with air vents that caught the odor, and the tank, caught the waste, it was always filled with water, a pail of waster was dumped in every few days. The tank was pumped by a special truck that would come by and pump it about once or twice a year.

All of the about 40 families in Peacock had outside restrooms. When I was a child. At least all of the folks I can remember.

In about 1½, years the Good Lord willing I will 90 years old. Peacock Michigan was a good little town for a child to grow up in, get a good country experience. I mean country, real country. Peacock only had 2 stores, one would usually close in the winter. The stores didn't have much in them anyway, but they had essential items like bacon, some meat, a few canned items, some drinks like soda, in a big container with legs on it with ice to keep the bottles like coca-cola, pepsie cola etc. cool in the summer winters no problem. It used to get down to near 25-30 below zero year's ago liquids would freeze in those temperatures if not protected, people too, got very cold.

We kept our old hand pumps protected, but those outside usually froze if the cylinder that raised the water from the ground, was not 4 to 6 ft beneath ground level protected with straw or someway protected from the real cold weather. The cylinder would freeze and had to be thawed to get the handle to raise the mechanism in the cylinder up and down when the handle was pumped to pump water.

People were used to that and made arrangements to protect their pumps because people need water. Folks also had small pumps inside their homes, usually near a sink, called pitcher pumps, they were only about 24 inches high with a handle that would operate a cylinder mechanism inside the pump and pump water from about 20 feet in the ground.

To install a pump in those days when I was living in Peacock about 80 years ago its now March of 2018 that was about 1935 or near that year. A pipe had to be driven in the ground on the end of the water pipe usually about 2 inches in diameter a person got a piece of pipe called a point it was a pointed pipe with a special point that could be driven in the ground when screwed to a longer piece of pipe. The pipe usually came in about 10 foot length's or longer that were threaded to be screwed together with couplings, and a metal cap to protect the pipe threads. Then the pipe was hammered in the ground with a sledge hammer one would hammer about 15 or 20 feet of pipe in the ground drop a piece of string with a small nut or bolt on it to check for water. When about 3 feet depth of water was struck,. screw on the pump you were in business. If you wanted a large pump with the cylinder below the ground dig a hole around the pipe to the depth desired then screw on the pump. Pitcher pumps no problem leave the pipe high placed on a little stand outside, or put it in a kitchen. More about the point of the pipe I spoke of to be driven the ground, it was made of heavy metal screwed to a piece of water pipe.

The point was about 3 feet long with small holes with something like small screen to keep the dirt out but let water in. This was driven in the ground when water was struck, the pipe would fill with water a hand pump could be installed to pump water. People also used windmills to operate the pump handle to pump water. Some places still use windmills way out on large acres of ground with cattle, to pump water, for the cattle to drink.

Most people now attach an electric pump to the pipe to raise water. I spent a lot of time explaining about obtaining water because water is very important and always has been. When my father got the little piece of ground we lived on it was very, very important to get water because Peacock Michigan had no running water. I think it still doesn't have running water each person had to have their own source of water. Way back then, when they obtained a piece of ground they had to build a house from whatever material they could afford. Install a pump for water and home living could begin. But they had to have water, people can't live without water.

Some other things I can remember growing from about 4 or 5 years old with my brother sister Father Mother and friends.

I remember the little one room school house, it was right across the gravel road (there was only one gravel road) thorough Peacock only about 35 or 40 people lived there at that time, about 1935.

Our old school the one room school, had or was a 2 story building with a rope operated bell on top of the building. The rope extended to the bell on top of the building thorough the top floor used for church on Sundays. The second floor was also used for school function's like Christmas programs or activities.

I can remember our little house Father made of railroad crossties I was born in that house grew up there, went to school from there. The schoolhouse was right across the gravel road about 200 yards from my front door. I went there till the 6th grade, Then we were sent to Brethren, Michigan to Dickson High School. Peacock elementary school was closed because there was not enough children in Peacock to keep the school operating. My 6th,7th, and 8th grades were at Dickson High School. I graduated from Dickson High School, Brethren Michigan in 1947.

I can remember the childhood years spent in Peacock though. They were good years spent with my brother, sister, family, friends, we had much fun in Peacock even though it was so small with not many people. There were a few children, we played together, went to school together rode our bicycles together, walked through the country roads, much of the country areas, visited the little Manistee River its little bridge. Also visited a little lake called Lost Lake on a little hill and many other places. Seen many animals like the many deer, rabbits, squirrel, birds, night hawks, owls, even snakes, frogs, and skunks. Dusty gravel roads, little sand trails, helped our parents, grow little gardens, harvest them. Like picking beans, corm, tomatoes, done all this together my family, friends and I.

When I got old enough at the old age of 14 years got my drivers license. I got an old auto a 1932 model B Ford for the vast sum of $15.00. Traded it, and for a sum of $75.00 gor a 1937 Ford in terrible shape, with my brothers help we pulled and overhauled the engine fixed the transmission which had a broken cluster gear in it. Getting much mechanical experience, from friends and a manual ordered from the Sears catalog. But Got the 37 Ford working good. Then traded it for a 1937 Willys sedan used it for I think my last 2 years of high school. Then traded it for a model A Ford for the engine to fix a model A Ford truck my mother had. Later I repaired the old truck engine put it in the model A car used it for about 1 or 2 days and went in the army, about 2 weeks after high school graduation in May 1947. Stayed in the army for 25 years and about 2 months. Retired from the army June 1972 entered the army May 27, 1947.

It is now March 23, 2018 those were all good years, learning years, of course we make mistakes, along the way but learn from them, keeps life interesting, The Creator has been good very good thru the years, gave me a family, life, much.

Thanks Creator and Bye,

Albert E. Vicent

Me, Albert Vicent

Haruko, our place, living room.

A PATTERN

Seems like no matter what we do, there's a certain pattern we follow to get it done. We seldom do things on the spur of the moment unless it's absolutely necessary. Even then we may quickly, very quickly refer to the sub consciousness for a little quick info and then act in the way we deem best.

In other words most things we do are done in the way we have somewhere done or seen something similar done we can refer back too to accomplish a present task. Even our animals, work animals, pets etc. after having observed them for a period we pretty much can determine how they will react if required to do certain things.

We use a certain tool to perform a certain task, usually because of that tools performance for us on a similar task, we have used it on in the past, and the list goes on.

This may not be true in all situations, but in some it perhaps may. Many may disagree. Call me sometime we can talk about it (ha-ha).

Now I must get back to something I have in mind the book title, its connection to many of my memoirs. The title 'The Room of¼ Where¼' The room is a portion of our living room, because it's being the room where, much of the memoirs were written. It was readily available for my little Casio digital camera to click a quick cover picture of the room of my now thoughts. Like some of the things I've recalled was like the items with reference to my Father his sitting a lot in his restful moments in his rocking chair. I recalled of an old rocker we had. I used to have a little rocking chair too, that sit close to my father's chair talked to him a lot of times, with my little Teddy Bear. I couldn't find a small rocking chair so I sit a Teddy Bear I borrowed in the rocking chair placed it in the picture click and it was instantly there returned instantly forever. Our children, not there in picture are there in memory because as I have listed most of the memoirs were written sitting on the love seat type little sofa with my feet propped across the little folding stool you can see where I always concealed it when finished under the plant (The large green plant at the end of the coffee table most near the love seat type sofa). I would always sit on writing with the black futon pillow placed on top of the stool, which would make the stool just the right height to give hours and hours of just pure imagery and quiet time stories, poetry, and all to surface and be caught with my ready pen then appear on paper. I say pen because I'm a hunt and peck typist, someone else does that part but I'll get better with time perhaps. Will be 90 years old in a month good lord willing, can't see me becoming a speed typist by then maybe sometime before the next 90 years finish (maybe) who knows (ha-ha). Lots of pens anyway and this Cross pen I'm using works fine.

The picture on the wall over the large sofa is of a crane we got it in Okinawa when I was stationed there while in the Army. The family was there with me except for a few months for nearly 9 years we were there, most of the children's growing, remembering years we really liked that place. It was and is still only about 60 miles long and 15 miles wide but we would always put about 10,000 miles per year on the auto because we were always going somewhere on off duty time, to the beach sightseeing or somewhere. The people spoke Japanese and pret-ty good English, My wife-Japanese, with my broken Japanese and English and the children speaking too. Children pick up language real quick. We had no trouble. Most every year we would go to Japan to visit the wife's relations on vacation or they would come visit. Japan and Okinawa are close. So those were good times. We'll always remember.

The coffee table came from Taiwan a friend of mine picked it up for me he always went own there on assignments and picked it up along with some other furniture items we still have. That's been years ago, because I retired from the military in June of 1972 and this is 2009 and that was maybe 1969, I served 2 tours in Okinawa. My friend settled in Colorado Springs. We visited him there about 3 or 4 years ago, his daughter called that he had passed away about 2 or 3 days ago. He was in his mid 80's my old army buddy, not many old timers left. We spent a lot of time on Okinawa and in the states together. We were together in Redstone Arsenal Alabama, Ft. Dix New Jersey. Our Children, same schools pretty much too. Except in Alabama, when we were there integration had not yet happened we could go all over the base together but the children had to go to different schools, could play go to military places, lived in the same housing on base, but in town it was that way then. People down there treated us nice though, at that time that was the way things were. Never been back since then. That was in the 1960's.

The little white looking spots on the crane picture, are little flowers. The dark spots are trees. A tree is on each side of the crane. The crane is standing among flowers looking up. If you look close you can get the idea. Cranes are kind of special birds in the Orient. They can be found in several pictures and paintings, mentioned in stories, poetry, etc.

The living room is my restful room I enjoy sitting by that window. Lots of light there, natural light. I try to do most writing using natural light, some at night, most by day. I turn on that white tall halogen light to finish. When dark slips in, it gives off good light.

Imagery of family members are in this room, I guess that's why these memoirs were so easy to write about. Must close, wife was listening to the TV. It just went off. I got the message it's near supper time. Get in here or hear about it. So must close for now.

Bye.

VACATION, CAMPING, ETC.

When we went on vacations was always happy times, especially when the children were young, and we had to travel far to our vacation destination. We went thru a lot on the way. Of course at the time, it required a lot of patience and at times seemed terrible, but bearable, and now that we look at it from a different point of view, we're proud it happened as it did. Be- cause getting there and back and the experiences on the way, for experiences are what makes up a memorable time.

Also when the children were young we would usually travel far. Like from Tacoma, Washington to Peacock, Michigan to visit my mother on a 30 day vacation. Driving an old 3 speed 53 Ford auto with 3 children and the wife. Many of the highways then were gravel too, bumpy and dusty. Believe it or not, we always made it with no car trouble of any kind. Oops, I'll take that back. With my old 65 Falcon Ford I remember the right rear Tire that was a recap tire gave out but put the spare on and away we went. No other trouble. And the old 53 Ford, after we had retained it for about 12 years, taken it to Okinawa for 6 years, drove it over there. The natives over there would do almost anything to an auto very reasonable. So before we brought it back, we had it painted, took the engine out at a hobby shop put in a lot of new parts, The car had about 150,000 miles on but the engine still didn't require too much, but the price was right so we done what was necessary and the engine performed beautiful. Put in new clutch, throw out bearing and all went thru the brake system. Had the car repainted, reupholstered, everything. New water pumps, that old v-8 engine had 2 water pumps, everything was ok. But I forgot to have the radiator cleaned so it reminded me when we started across country to my new assignment with the family to Aberdeen Proving Grounds in Maryland. Had to have the radiator replaced, otherwise no trouble.

The old 53 Ford was really a good car. A friend on base bought it from me when I purchased the 65 Falcon Ford that we also took on a return assignment to Okinawa and he drove the old 53 Ford to Wisconsin.

When we traveled, with the children as they were growing, we had to be cost conscious thoughtful and all because, when young, raising a family, you have to do that.

Traveling with the old 53 Ford I had rigged the back of the driver's seat (the old car was a 4 door sedan). Anyway, I had rigged the back of the front seat so it could be lowered to make the entire car into a bed, a lot of times on a long trip we would pull into a rest stop late at night make the car into a bed, sleep, wake up, get out the (usually a sterno–heater) used a lot then called canned heat, a little can with a pasty smelling alcohol substance that would burn. You could then fry eggs and bacon with a little folding stand that came with it quite easily. Get milk or juice from the cooler we always carried, eat and be on our way. Every other evening we might stay in a motel we could afford. The next morning and be on our way. Sometimes I would also with the old 53 Ford because the engine was designed so I could do it, purchase canned food that each person wanted and set the cans on different parts of the engine. Drive maybe 50 or 75 miles before we wanted to eat and usually when we got to the time for the meal, things would be hot. And if a can fell out, we would joke about it and share food till next time, makes good memories. We still talk about it at times.

Mother's house didn't have inside plumbing; outside Toilet, hand pump and the works, even a wood burning cook stove. So the kids had experience of priming and pumping a hand pump for a pail of water. Priming a pump is when water is poured into the pump if needed to moisten the little cylinder mechanism that goes up and down when the handle is moved to start the water flow raise water from the ground below to the pail. The children got the experience.

Also they got experience of seeing a wood and coal burning stove. Also an outside toilet. We even had to move the toilet one time for mother to new spot, we have pictures of the move, where the excrement hole is covered a new hole dug, the building moved. Set in place and presto you are in business again. That's the way things were done when they had to be done that way.

When visiting in the winter in the little country town in Michigan where mother lived the children got to see the snow and even experience cutting their little Christmas tree of choice dragging it home erecting a stand and decorating it. That was fun.

We also went to Niagara Falls near New York one Time. Erected a pole type tent an experience the family had, together, they later became Cub Scouts when I became a Cub Scout Master while in Okinawa, an experience that was to last 2 weeks that terminated over 3 years later. But raising children those times must be shared and performed, by parents. Charles, raised both of his boys later to be Eagle Scouts. He became Scout Master-for several years. From that tenting trip well who knows but that's where it could have started. The vacations', raising a family was fun. It had its rough spots too, but with communication, open minds, that's what it takes to make the trip enjoyable and memorable, on the way thru.

Bye for now. Got to go. Its suppertime.

P.S.

As the children got older, had families of their own Charles got a trailer, I purchased and old dodge motor home, we refurbished kept it at Charles Place he has an acre of ground we used take everyone and go camping together. One Time we went to Oregon. Had a good time.

I still have an old VW Pop Top camper, had many good camping experiences with it. Really enjoy vacations and camping.

Bye again.

P.S.S.

Almost forgot this little item, since this memoir is about vacations and this is also important to me, anyway, since it still pop's up in memory from time to time. It's my return from Japan on my first time of having went there in Jan. 1948 at the young age of 18 and this was the completion of my first army enlisting of 3 years which would count on my 25 years of service, when I retired from the army in 1972

I remember because of a Kidney problem that developed on the return trip. We traveled by ship, then it took about 3 weeks to get back from Japan. We landed in Washington State and I went to a military hospital in Tacoma stayed there for some time. My tonsils were re- moved was told that had caused the problem, some kind of infection.

My enlistment terminated there. I reenlisted for another 3 years, that's when the fun started all over again. Imagine an adventurous 20 year old, with 30 days furlough to spend wherever, a reenlistment bonus, and lots of energy. Of course having been away from home for nearly 3 years I wanted to see my home town again. After all was ok, found out where my new assignment was I was to report back to Camp Stoneman in California.

I then left on my furlough to Peacock Michigan. Seen my mother, brother, sister rela- tion, friends and all, found the old vehicles I so patiently fixed were there no more. Have to have a vehicle can't have a vacation without wheels, so the next day I think I went with my brother on my way to purchase a vehicle. At that time servicemen had to wear the uniform everywhere so when boarding the bus the driver asked. "Hi soldier boy where you headed."

Told him I was on vacation and was looking for a cheap good old car. I remember he said "Ok maybe I can help you", seemed bus drivers who daily operate thru small towns know what's going on. So when we got to this one little gas station the bus driver told me "Hey soldier boy, check with the station operator he might have a car."

The station operator seemed like a nice person greeted me with, "Hi Corporal, how's everything." Sounded like another GI in fact, so did the bus driver. I soon found out the station operator had just gotten out of the military and had purchased that station. I informed him I was on 30 day furlough and wanted a cheap good 30 day car. He told me had just taken in pretty good old car had checked it over handed me the keys said go look at it, take it for a spin. The bus driver said he had to be there for a few minutes don't be to long he could wait. So I checked the auto out. All was ok informed the station operator. He informed me to give him I think it was $65.00 and the car was mine. Paid him, thanked the bus driver we waved at each other. The bus went on its way. Signed the Title, filled the gas tank. Shook hands. The service station man told me "Have a good furlough Corporal.", and believe me I did. That was a good old 1935 V8 Ford. It never gave any trouble. I went everywhere with it. Everywhere in the area I even thought I wanted to go. Seen all my old hi-school friends. Even went way out in the country to a little lake called lost lake, and caught a little fish about 8 in, long, but threw it back. Just had a good old time.

Then when the 30 days was nearly finished with enough time to get back to my new base on time, drove my old 35 Ford to Baldwin Left it for my brother to pick up. Got on the bus, to further adventure at Camp Stoneman, California, Which included my quickly finding a Heavy Trucking unit headed for the Far East needing another mechanic and away I went again to adventures that included The Korean War, Later marriage, family, and a military experience of 25 years. But that 1950 furlough, the old 1935 Ford V8, seeing the family, being 20 years old, also see- ing our dog Skippy whom also after 3 years never forgot me, and another time of nearly 5 years never forgot me. Till he passed away, was too an experi- ence. Adventure is great, and memories are too. Had to mention this.

Bye again.

Haruko cooking hot dogs at Toro Park, Salinas, Ca.
And my old 1977 yellow VW van my favorite vehicle.

THE PICKLE STATION

About the middle of July or the first part of August, I think, is when folks that lived in little towns around Lake Country Mich. Would start to bring in cucumbers they raised to the Squire Dingee Pickle Station in Peacock. The station was between Gales Store and Allen's Church. It was painted dark off red color and had big letters painted in white on the side of it, Squire Dingee you could read the name from the old gravel road as you passed by, I used to read the letters when I passed by going to Gales or Comstock's Store They were the only stores in Peacock and Comstock's Store usually closed in the winter, so we only had the one in winter.

The station also had a sign with its name on it in front of the station facing the railroad track. Because there was a piece of the side track of the railroad track that was made over close to the pickle station where a train car that looked kind of like an oil car trains pull to carry liquids only this one held cucumbers. The station had a wooden ramp where people could walk over to the car from the pickle station and dump pickles into the car that were taken in at the station, from the farmers. It was pretty busy in the late summer during cucumber harvest.

It was especially interesting when it started its annual operations, because Peacock was always quiet, there was no noise except a car passing by and there wasn't many cars then. Sometime a motorcycle, about 2 trains, the freight and the passenger. Other than that no other sounds except local folk sounds of about 40 people and they lived about 3/4 of a mile apart so you didn't hear much. But if someone talked loud, and they were outside and angry it carried thru the country air quite well.

But still when the old pickle station opened and folks came in with their cucumbers from patches of ground usually from about 1/4 acre to 3-4-5 acres of cucumbers or more the old pickle station was busy.

It was interesting, I've never forgotten the old Squire Dingee pickle station from when started to learn the alphabet. I would practice my letters at times when I walked by and check my choice of letters with someone in the know, to see if my choice of letters was correct. Whenever I walked by the letters were always there to check my knowledge on until I got the alphabet in my mind well, all the letters. I've never forgotten that the pickle station had a cu- cumber sorting machine that was brought out from inside the building to a large open covered wooded platform about 20x25ft square this sorter had places where different sized pickles could fall from different areas of the machine. The farmers would dump the pickles into a place on one end of the machine. They would then be shuffled along by the machines internal working parts and fall into little boxes where they would be weighed and the farmer paid for his labor by the various sized cucumbers he brought in. Then the pickles were loaded onto, I think, wheelbarrows or other forms of transportation, taken up the ramp and dumped into the train pickle car. When the car was full the train would pick it up and bring another car until the cucumber season finished.

This sorting machine was operated by a gasoline engine, because Peacock didn't have electricity then. I think the old engine was a Fairbanks Morse engine I can remember it had a large external very heavy looking fly wheel on it with a pulley and a little belt connected to the pickle sorting machine and when the engine was running, I really liked to watch it because you could see it sitting there just putt, putt, putt, putting. It intrigued me because I really liked mechanical things. We at that time had nothing with a gasoline engine, couldn't afford it, and here was this engine just sitting there working sorting the pickles and making a strange sound it would fire putt, then the flywheel being very heavy compared to engine size would carry the engine thru its next revolution if it wasn't under load a few strokes it might fire one putt, then coast for a few revolutions then fire one or two time's putt, putt then coast again. If a lot of pickles came thru it would fire continuously as long as it was working hard sounding putt, putt, putt, putt. This was really interesting to me, I really liked to watch that machine in operation. It's interesting even now years later when I think about it. I feel it really helped shape my in- terests in auto and other related mechanical things as I grew thru the years. I also can remember a little oil container mounted on the engine to lubricate some part of the engine. It was made of glass or some material. Because you could see the oil inside, it was usually about 1/2 full I used to watch it too, and wonder when it would become empty and what would happen if it did. It never did become empty though. It must have been checked closely by the station operator. This putt, putt, putt of the pickle station engine was a welcome noise in Peacock during its seasonal operations.

When it was put away for the winter or when the season finished for the year we children would play on the platform. I remember in our school the pencil sharpener was mounted on the window sill facing the railroad track the pickle station was there, and you could see it. I used to look at it when sharpening my pencil. I think the old station was there when I went in the army. Of course it's gone now.

I'll never forget the cucumber season. The people bringing in the cucumbers with horse wagons, various types of old cars, trucks. We had a small plot of cucumbers, and having no vehicle, brought our little bags of cucumber in on fathers little push cart. We always made a few coins though not much for the work involved, but we learned from it. Working in a cucumber field, picking cucumbers, dragging a bag of cucumbers in the hot muggy sun is hard, very hard work. But it must be done, and if one makes a living that way, its honest work.

The old Peacock Squire Dingee Pickle Station.

I wish we had a picture of it but very few folks had cameras then, we certainly didn't. So no pictures only memories.

Good memories.

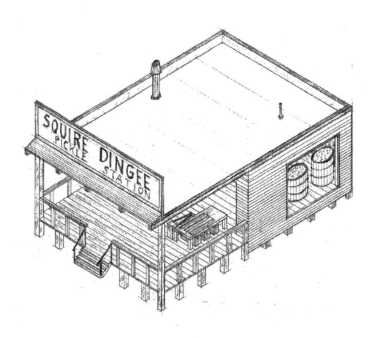

This is what my memory tells me it looked like.

SUMMER, WINTER, STOVES, SNOWPLOWS

The summers were always hot, humid and muggy. Days and nights, about the same temperature wise. Of course living in that area one gets climatized, it's accepted. We're comfortable now with air conditioners and being here in this part of California, Salinas where the climate nearly always' pretty much ok. But in Peacock it was different back then. In the summer evenings always brought out mosquitoes and it seemed they all liked me, no one had mosquito repellant. I remember the bites made the areas bitten swelled, itched. Later the swelling would go away. But mosquitoes still like me. My father would burn rags to drive away the mosquitoes. It worked pretty good, but oh, the smoke was bothersome.

The winters were always cold, real cold. Our house wasn't very well insulated. It was not unusual for snow to be blown thru cracks in the mornings. If it was near your bed so be it, it was there, get used to it, and we did. The fire would soon warm the house (the room you were in). When the heating stove got to roaring like wood and coal fires do.

At night the fires were let to burn out. Sometime when all the drafts on the stove are closed. Drafts are sliding little doors built to let the fire burning in the stove have more air. To burn bigger or higher put out more heat if the draft or vent is opened more or if the vent is slid more in the closed position it burns more low. The fuel is not consumed so rapid. There is also a vent that can be turned left or right in the pipe leading from the stove to outside the house carrying smoke from the fire outside. This vent can also be turned. When turned left or right by its little control handle outside the pipe that moves a disc or flapper inside the pipe left or right to let more or less air thru because it lets the main source of air come to the stove.

If it is nearly closed and the stove vents closed also the stove fire with a lot of fuel burning low, lasts a long time. Sometimes all night depending on the type of fuel used. If the fire goes out and no one gets up to put fuel on the fire the house is cold in the morning and without central heating, no electric or gas, you have to build another fire in the stove or fireplace (which works nearly the same as a stove).

In the winter also, I used to like to watch the snow plows plow the snow going past our house. Our house was near the one gravel road going thru Peacock.

The snowplow would be mounted on front of the truck, and the truck would usually have sand or something heavy in the bed of the truck and chains on the tires, so it could push heavy snow to open the roads if there had been a big blizzard and much snow had fallen. When real blizzard weather came schools would close, if they were open and the bus, when our Peacock school closed, that took us about 30 miles away to Dickson High School in Brethren Michigan. If bad weather came the school bus would bring us home early. Sometime there would be no school for 2 or 3 days if the storm continued.

I always liked to watch the snowplows when the truck came by pushing the snow. The plow was usually always mounted on an angle from the driver side of the plow to push the snow a little forward and off the passenger's side, that way the pushed snow as the truck moved forward would be thrown to the side of the road. Another truck going the other way or the same vehicle on its return trip would open the other side of the road.

As the truck went by it would be moving pretty fast throwing snow it was always fun to watch. We would say, there goes the snow plow, maybe there will be school tomorrow. So we would go down to our neighbor who had an old hand crank type phone to see if a call had come for school to reopen.

There was one snowplow I always liked to see go by it was an old truck that for some reason, I don't know why, had a wooden cab on it. Someone said it had been damaged while nearly new and the wood cab had been put on it. It also had chains to make it move, moving over the inside of the tires on big sprockets on each of the rear wheels powered by little turning sprockets about or near back of the truck cab. This made me think of a bicycle, and that maybe I could make a truck. Because we didn't have a car for a long time, I thought, gosh, something like that should not be too hard to make. I really liked to watch that old truck go by. It was neat. The trucks used to also be mounted with a scraper usually about midway under the truck. It would go by scraping the dirt roads leveling chuck holes also the gravel roads, in the spring after melting snow and frost from the winter and after big rain storms.

When the roads were black topped then a lot of the scraping was not needed.

It was also fun to watch the old steam train with their snowplows. They were usually of a v type plow placed in front of the locomotive pushing snow off the railroads, left and right sides as the train went speeding by throwing snow high in the air while black smoke from the old steam train also permeated the air. I can almost smell it now the smoky odor smell from a long freight train with sometime, 2 locomotives, one to pull the other to help on hills of a long freight train both puffing it they stopped, to get rolling again was a sight to see and smell in the air. Haven't ever smelled anything with the odor of an old steam train since they are no more. The diesels aren't quite the same, they smell more like a bus going by. Oh another thing after the snow plows cleared the highways we had to re-shovel our house paths because they got filled with snow when the snowplow went by. Interesting, this visit with Michigan summer, winter, snowplows and all. But¼ Gotta go now.

Bye.

SPENCER'S BRIDGE AND TRAIN MAIL PICK UP

*Dickson Rural Agricultural
School Buses
Lined up at Dickson School
Sept. 1938 Brethren, Mich.
1939Ford, 1937 Chevy, 1938 GMC,
1938 International, 1938 GMC,1937
International, 1932 Chevy and old
bus on the end made by a gentleman
who brought his children to school
in it every school day.
Buses were red white and blue then
instead of yellow in color. My
brother and I rode the 1939 Ford
Bus, on left side. For quite some time.*

THE ROOM OF RETURN

The walk down to Spencer's bridge was always nice, summer and winter because we always took the way we thought was best taking our time, usually, my brother I, and a few friends, we would go by their house and ask them. Most of us lived, let's see now, one friends house from our place was about ¾ mile away, another about a mile, the other 2 friends were about a mile away also.

So when we all got together as only one person had a telephone, it was the old hand crank kind. No one could answer, no one else had a telephone. Se we had to walk by and set up the planned excursion or ride a bike by, or walk by and ask if they could, or wanted to go along. The place was about 3 miles away. A nice walk, we were all children then of age from 6 thru 11 or 12 years of age and our parents would trust us on a country walk after our chores were finished. Mr. Spencer once was postmaster in Peacock.

We would usually leave after a noon meal, maybe take a bread and butter sandwich for snack take our time, walk take in the usual country sights in the summer of animal tracks, discuss which type animal made which track, like a squirrel, or a cat, a twisting slither we knew was a snake, and to be wary if it was large or fairly large because the predator that made the track might be near, with its friend, or friends. These tracks could be seen, because most of the roads off the main gravel road were wagon trail type roads made by wagons or car tires. When autos used them too made the trails a little wider and deeper so there was about an 8 or10 inch track on each side with grassy area between. The same width one can see when an automobile drives on a beach and leaves a track, that is what was seen all over the county made by horses and wagons. Later used by automobiles and people walked these trails rode horses, bikes, motorcycles or whatever to commute. They were later made into wider roads.

But on them we could see tracks of animals or whatever to make our walk and visit interesting, Spencer's bridge was named after a gentleman that had a small farm near the little river that was in that vicinity and a small bridge was built over it. The bridge was maybe 50 or 75 ft. long. Wagons could pass over it and for some reason it picked up the name of Spencer's Bridge, which it is still today, years later, called.

The river was of clear, very clear water you could most always, if you looked close, see small, sometimes large, fish or a snake swim by in the river. Or maybe if someone that lived near the river might cross with their horse and wagon, stop and chat with us and be on their way. While we boys just visited, threw stones in the water, enjoying ourselves.

Sometime if we were finished, if someone's horse and wagon were large enough and there wasn't too many children say only 3 or 4 we would hitch a ride back on the wagon if our neighbor was going that far.

That was always fun because the horse went slow, and you could watch the wagon wheels turn slow round and round. Sometimes if the horse was pretty gentle the neighbor would let you hold the reins and actually drive the horse and wagon. You pulled left rein for the horse to turn left, the right rein for the horse to turn right. Hold both reins; pull back on them the horse would stop. There were also commands to give the horse like gee-haw, gid-yup - etc. Just driving steering like the neighbor would let us do on the country trail on our return from a visit to Spencer's Bridge was just fun to do because the neighbor knew the old gentle horse trusted a little child to drive while he was near, knew the old trail and the horse was maybe happy to feel the reins held and maybe happy to hear children's voices.

When we got back we had to stop by the little post office, pick up the mail we would always step into the little post office part where there was a big wooden box with a glass front. The box or glassed in area was maybe 6 ft by 5 ft with a little compartment for each family you knew where your compartment was. The postmaster had the name on his side, he would shove the letters in the compartment, you could look and see if you had mail or ask.

If the train had not yet came or there was no reason for it to stop at the depot a lonesome but interesting thing would happen. Lonesome because the train would not stop in little Pea- cock a little town of only about 40 people. When the old steam engine stopped there was always a little excitement all the steam from the puffing old engines, smoke from its smoke stack. Big wheels on the engine and fire in engine, if you were close you could see, when the fire man would throw coal in the fire for heat for the engine. That was rare to witness, but a steam train was always interesting to me. I liked them and missed something when they did not stop.

The interesting thing to witness when the train did not stop for someone to hand the baggage car outgoing mail, was the way it was picked up, I think it was called "on the fly" or (pickup on the fly). The train would not stop, it might slow a little, but it would whistle for the railroad crossing which was near where the little train stop was, but go by quite fast. The mail bag was hung on special post that was of a very silvery color, with a special place to hang the bag so it could be dislodged easily. The train would speed by with an extended arm, pickup the mail bag from the post, and that was it. Mail pick up for the day from Peacock by the mail train for that day was accomplished. On our way back from our little trip to Spencer's Bridge was a frequent trip interesting, and for a haunting reason I seem to always remember.

The days in Peacock to me are always nice to remember. Especially the little walks to Spencer's Bridge. Another place was Lost Lake a little lake about 3 miles from Peacock on a little hill, or seemed to be. Nothing was there but the little lake but it was a nice walk. Another place was a place called Bloody Row where we were told a logging train turned over many years before our time in Peacock injuring many people it was maybe about 5 miles away between Peacock and a little town called Bass Lake and it too, was nice little walk.

There were several little places like that, nice little experiences that filled empty moments, and passed the fast moving years by.

AUTOS, TRUCKS, ETC

The old steam train used to come thru the little Michigan town where I lived, there was a freight train in the morning about 8 or 9 am. Then a passenger train about noon. The freight would sometimes switch cars to the side track and sometime leave cars if something was to be left like rail road cross ties or something. I remember some people that came from Jamaica. They were not very big in stature but the very heavy crosstie's soaked with creosote a black oil, looking substance to slow the ties from spoiling in the ground.

These people would put a piece of cloth on their shoulder place the tie on their shoulder and walk a little ramp from the railroad boxcar containing the ties stack them on a pile of ties and continue however long it took to unload the cars. Very strong little men. When they finished they would soon disappear there was nothing in Peacock not even, electric lights or inside plumbing. Just our small population town, of about 40 people. The most nearby little town was called Baldwin, in about 1935-1940 era, it had about a 600 people population. But it did have electric lights and running water. Maybe they stopped there.

As time passed along my brother was getting older we did not have a car, never had one, had to depend on others who had a car to get to Baldwin to purchase needed items. The train would stop in Peacock, sometimes we would ride the train to town purchase items and come back on the train. That was quite difficult to do, and carry many items that way.

There were two little stores in Peacock but they didn't have much.

Sometimes I remember riding to Baldwin in our neighbors horse and wagon. It was only 12 miles each way, but by horse and wagon it took quite a while.

When my brother got old enough to get a driver's license my mother bought an old car. I remember it was a 1931 Chevrolet 2 door sedan. I think she paid $40.00 for it from a gasoline station owner in town. She knew nothing about a car, but she

20

bought it. Having very little money she bought it on an installment plan. It took her a long time to pay for that old car, but she finally paid for it.

My brother had already gotten his license or got them after we got the car, because I can remember an old man that knew how to drive a car showing my brother how to use the clutch and brake pedal and shift the gears. My brother soon got the understanding down and we had a car. A means to get out of Peacock, when we wanted to. It was a pretty good old car too.

I can't remember it ever giving any real serious trouble except when we first got it, it stopped running and was pushed in our yard. My brother in law came by and took off the fuel pump, said he learned how to do it while in the CCC, Civilian Conservation Corp. Which was used to give folks jobs while the big depression was going on, but by the late 1930's times was getting better. Anyway my brother-in-law learned how to take off fuel pumps and clean them which was what our old 1931 Chevrolet at that time needed, because it started pumping gasoline back up to the engine, it started, and never did give any trouble like that again.

I remember the starter quit working but you could insert a crank in the car right at the bottom of the radiator, in those days, and crank the engine by hand cranking it and get in and drive away, which we continued to do with the old Chevrolet as long as I remember our owning it. Several people cranked automobiles then. My brother and I still wanted something to haul wood with the Chevrolet with a trailer was ok a neighbor had one available for use most anytime. But a pickup was desired, without much mechanical knowledge or money, trading for one of almost any value as a dependable vehicle living in an isolated spot like peacock was not wise.

Guess what happened, my brother and I found an old 1923 or 24 pickup a Dodge Brothers it was called then, before the vehicle carried the name Dodge only. It was very old, had a 4 cylinder engine, it did not even have a fuel pump, it had what was known as a vacuum tank to bring fuel from the tank at rear of the vehicle to the engine, not to dependable. The vehicle had been sitting for quite some time. That didn't matter, we had seen it and wanted it because it was a truck. We convinced mother to sign the papers. The trade was made and that was a big mistake, because the truck we soon found had big engine troubles. The engine must have frozen in cold weather or gotten to hot and cracked something inside the engine because water would leak into the engine oil and truck could not be used. So we were without a vehicle again back to square one, where we were before my brother got his driver's license

The other man was happy he had a pretty good old car. We later found out he was a pretty good mechanic also. We had a lot to learn. This big auto trade took place in late summer or early fall, can't remember the year. I do remember we went all that winter with no automobile and could see our mistake. That old truck all covered with snow sitting reminding us of what should not have happened. My brother got angry and threw a brick through the windshield and radiator of the old truck, I kind of felt sorry for the old truck then.

During the winter one of our friends was discharged from the military. Second world war was going on then tires, gasoline and all were rationed he purchased the front axle and all even though the old truck had wood spoke wheels on it he adapted it to his car and used the front axle and tires. The old truck was later sold for junk.

The following spring and summer still having no vehicle and little almost no money my brother had drivers license, we had to make money someway. Peacock with its about 40 residents had no work, but it had two little stores and Peacock was located in Lake County near several lakes where many people had cabins near the little rivers and lakes they came to visit in spring and summer. They would come to the stores and buy strawberries and blueberries we called then huckleberries, they grew wild in the country and strawberries grew good along the railroad track where the steam trains ran because they would puff out steam as they rolled along their tracks watering the various berries. So we picked and picked berries that summer picked enough to buy an old 1934 Ford V-8 Tudor Sedan for $65.00 it was a pretty good old car we were rolling again.

Not long after that I became a teenager and got my drivers license at age 14 with my mother's permission. My brother and I were determined to learn more about mechanics which we did. I met friends in high school that had helped their fathers work on autos thru talking with them and auto books we purchased we learned much. I purchased a 1932 Ford from a neighbor at the grand old age of 15 years. Kept it for a little while, it only cost $15.00. Then I traded it and got a 1937 Ford Sedan. It was in terrible shape, the engine smoked the transmission had a broken tooth and clicked in low gear. But it was great for ambitious young people to experiment with so my brother and I pulled the engine out. Tore it all apart ground the valves, put in a set of piston rings, and insert's. Connecting red bearings, main bearings, a rebuilt clutch disc and clutch throw out bearing. Took the transmission apart and put in a cluster gear, the old one had a tooth broken on low gear that's why it clicked. When we put the old car back together it ran real good, you could hardly hear it run.

I put new sealed beam lights on it too, because the old cars then had bulb type headlights that were not very bright, sealed beam lights were just coming out. You could purchase a kit to do the job with. Believe it or not most auto parts for the rebuilding we purchased from Sears catalogue, there were a lot of shady tree mechanics around then, not in Peacock though. Also replaced the vacuum windshield wiper with an electric wiper, on the 1937 Ford. Got it from Sears.

I later traded the 1937 Ford for a 1937 Willys sedan which was also a good car I ran it for about 2 years then traded it for a model a Ford sedan that I needed the engine out of to put in a model A Ford truck we had purchased. I wanted to fix it so my brother could use it to haul things with because I was going into the army when I finished high school which was in about 1 or 2 months, the truck had a bad engine. Any way I changed engines in the vehicles fixed the old engine out of the truck and put it in the car. Made a last trip to Baldwin to see all my friends there and I think, the next day left to go in the army to stay for 25 years and 1 or 2 months and, that was years ago (May 1947-June 1972). Had so much fun, especially with the old cars. Never will forget 'em.

OLD AUTO'S AND WINTER

In Michigan, about October, it starts getting cool the leaves start changing, trees are simply beautiful many people especially out of state people just drive thru the country just viewing the changing leaves on trees.

Our Daughter Nicky and Haruko at our place.

Mariko Kanna, Haruko and her mother.

Of course the weather is changing too from summer, to autumn, to winter, so, folks with autos have to get 'em ready reasonably quick because nights are getting cold.

Now there are much better products to perform that task with, years ago there wasn't much and the autos wasn't as advanced. Radiators wasn't too good, leaks were abundant. Antifreeze wasn't as advanced, or water hoses, autos heaters. A lot of folks including myself just ran water all year, get the old car started then add the water cover the radiator about half way and be on your way. When you got where you were going and the car was going to set for a long period of time drain the water, and refill before leaving. If one was shopping, starting and stopping, as long the engine was warm no problem. Engine oils then were not multi-grade. They were usually 10-20-30-40-50 etc. weight. The higher the number the more heavy the oil, when cold, got quite like grease. When the engine got cold about 18-20 below cars were at times hard to start. One had to remember to change to lighter weight oil. At times you could see folks make little fires under the engine oil pan to warm the oil hoping to start the engine, or place a pan of hot coals from the stove under the oil pan, do many odd things. Old cars in the winter not kept in good condition were very hard to start. Kept inside a building helped much.

Outside usually difficult when it got 20 or 30 below zero. For radiators alcohol a special blend was also used.

Engine oils the types now used and antifreeze coolants for auto engines are a big help for automobiles.

My brother and I had many very interesting, unforgettable days with our old autos. We laugh about it now but it wasn't really funny. Then because it gets really cold in Peacock Mich.

Heaters wasn't very good in autos then and most old cars didn't have any, unless some- body put one in. When a new car was purchased they were usually an extra cost item, especially on the cheaper autos.

Just thought I'd mention these items
Se Ya Later

IT STARTED

It all started in 1947. That was my last year of high school. Not too much else was circulating in my mind except regular teen age thoughts.

In my little Michigan town of Peacock of about 40 people not much happened almost everyone knew everyone and everything that was new, old too.

I had a little 1937 Willys car that I repaired, worked, and paid for all $75.00 and it was always taking me somewhere, after I finished my school work. I always made sure that was completed. I wasn't a star student, but my work was always done. My brother was somewhat of a brain with schoolwork, he would always help me with my chemistry, algebra, and geometry. He had finished high school several years before but still remembered how to do most everything but still would make me try all solutions before giving any assistance, which I could understand, and that was good.

After all my homework was completed, then being a teenager and no teenager's were in Peacock, my attention would be focused on my little old 1937 Willys auto which always seemed to be waiting. Mother and Father would usually ask "You going out tonight." Even my brother might ask, he was usually home evenings too. Kind of late isn't it. "It's only 8:30 or 9:00" I'd reply. I had that old wandering mind, had to go somewhere. Would tell everybody I'm just going to Baldwin, It was about 12 miles away. Father would usually say "Lad", he always called us lad, "remember go on your own hook, stay out of trouble, be careful". My father was an old man and was 80 years old when I was born, my mother was much younger though.

He himself had traveled much. His father, he said, was an Irishman and a plantation owner, his mother a slave. Said he was 13 years old when President Lincoln was running for office. He had a lot of history behind him. A lot of teachers that taught in the old Peacock school used to like to talk with him, because he knew and had witnessed much of the history they taught. I was too young to be aware of what was happening then, but can look back and marvel at it now. He also said he ran away to Canada at 13 years of age and acquired the name of Vicent. His fathers name was Patton.

He used to tell of much of his hunting and fishing experiences too. He knew how to make and set traps. Old Indian style traps, that very few people knew how to duplicate and if others seen them in the woods they knew who prepared it, and would tell father about it and if anything was in it. Father lived among Indian people for many years. Could speak some Indian language quite well, I think it was Chinook. Was a good shot with his shotgun even in his old age. My brother still has fathers old single shot 16 gage shotgun that father said he used to use in shooting matches.

I remember my father said when he was a teenager that a black panther had knocked him down and was about to scratch his intestines out with his rear legs and his father shot the panther, saving his life.

He also told of his fishing trips. He must have been quite a fisherman. He used to talk about the Puget Sound where he must have fished before, the Columbia River of sailboats, of tacking, something to do with sailboats. He also spoke of whaleboats cutting up whales, the blubber and things like that. He also spoke of small boats where a harpoon would be shot into the whale. He must have been on boats where that was done.

He always sat in a rocking chair that he would repair when broken even to making rockers for it. It was always near the stove. He made me a little rocking chair, that always was near his. We would always talk.

He made a lot of things, toys for we kids. Like jumping jacks he called them. You could squeeze the wooden handles, and a man he made of wood would be swung (by a twisted leather string he tanned from deer hide) back and forth over the string. He also made gates for people, made sleds for animals like horses to pull, fixed broken spokes in wagons wheels. There were lots of horses and wagons when we were young. My father was an interesting man. I really respected him, and my mother. They were wonderful people.

My Father passed away in March of 1947. I remember we were turning him over in the bed and he died in our arms. He said he was born, July 4th, 1850.

His name was William Vicent

My son's name too was William Henry Vicent. He too died in his early 40's while we stood around his bed. He too was a wonderful man. I will never forget our son.

Now back to where I first started this writing on Page #1 where I said it all started in 1947. It did, that was my senior year in high school. I remember right before or immediately after my father passed away, I think it was before though.

This army recruiting man came to our school. The teacher in one of our classes said this gentleman wanted to talk to the class. So the Sgt. gave his talk. He showed us pictures, talked, told us about the retirement if you stayed 20 years or more. About military schooling, about working in fields you might choose. Took names of those who chose to give them to him and left. No one mentioned anything about it again.

Then the month of May came around, lo and behold we graduated and it all started to sink in. Hey, schools finished, no more studying no more anything now what? Now what, all of a sudden no more anything, didn't seem so nice anymore. The old gray matter started thinking what am I going to do. Not many poor folks thought or even spoke much about college. Finishing high school was quite an accomplishment then, because not too many got that far. Now it's much different. But about a week later I was sitting on our front porch with my brother, and this army car stopped in front of our place. I recognized the Sgt. The same Sgt. that had talked to us in high school back in March.

He said "Hi Albert, remember me, ready to go." I said "Go where?". He said, "Go in the Army." "Go in the Army? Just like that?". He said "Yes, I can give you the test now. I have all the papers here". I said "Ok". I think he either waited in his car or sat down. I finished in a few minutes. He said to finish what I had to do, I had passed the test. I think I was either putting an engine in an old model A Ford truck, or did it soon after but anyway he came back picked me up about 2 weeks later, I went in the Army and stayed not only the 20 years the Sgt. told us you could retire after having completed, but for 25 years. Traveled the Far East, Japan, and Korea. Visited Taiwan, and spent a 9 years in Okinawa, spent some years in Alaska. Traveled about all over the United Stated. Married in Japan, raised a family. Retired from the military in1972, used my G.I. bill got my Associate of Arts Degree. Worked with the school district for 22 ½ years. Also, still work mornings with preschooler's, at a local Jr. College. The Creator has been good to me and I appreciate it. By trying to help others on the way. I try to show my appreciation. That's what we are supposed to do I think.

My Father
William Vicent
(1850-1947)
His carving of Paul Bunyan's Blue Ox
On the pole by him.
Peacock, Michigan

Received from Mom,
23ʳᵈ April 1951
In Pusan, Korea
(1890-1981)

Haruko and our granddaughters Haruka and Kanna at Charles
son's graduation UCLA (our grandson).

Charles son's graduation UCLA (our grandson)

TEDDY BEAR

Almost all things are interesting when you're a child, even the clouds on high, when they drift aimlessly by. Looking like something familiar. A child might let its feelings be known saying, that cloud over there looks like a rabbit. Many other things could be added to a child's list of imagination. Like a big red fire truck when it was just seen, or maybe that neat little toy car you can open the door get in. Close the door, steer and ¼ move by walking or moving your feet. Boy oh boy that could be fun, and if it was also painted to look like a Police Car, wow. Why if my friend had little truck and I had that car we can, and if we were on that big old place behind our house no one uses any more except kids "wow", now could we have just loads and loads of fun. Boy, oh boy, oh boy, oh boy. And the imaginary world of toys just goes on, and on, and on.

My one little toy that I really remember, and is at the top of the memory list. With many others but in a special, very special place. That it earned for good bear service by its very own self, is my Little Teddy Bear. I really liked that Little Bear, would take it almost everywhere with me. We would go in imaginary trips, have tea, eat, sleep together, take naps together, ride my little scooter car together, get scolded together.

My father was old man, he always respected my Teddy Bear, and would always listen while I related my Teddy Bear experience. My father would always listen no matter what he was doing. That connection, that father son bond always continued. Even when I was a teenager my father was always there listening, letting me express my thoughts, because when I was age 17, he was 97. He was a wonderful father. Back to my Teddy Bear, kind of got off track, pardon me. My father always connected the Teddy Bear, with Teddy Roosevelt. The President, because he was around when the bear came on the scene.

I think the Teddy Bear got its name and made its appearance mainly. Due to a hunting experience Teddy Roosevelt was on, and spared the life of a little bear cub.

Shortly after that incident the Teddy Bear entered the scene, and was, also still is, extremely popular.

For me it really was. I remember my little Bear and I would sometimes take imaginary trips to our own special places. On own little airplane, and ships. I remember one trip Teddy Bear and I took after I read a little book. They were small books very cheap to buy about maybe 3 inches square and maybe 2 inches thick. With one page large easy to read words, and a picture of the words next page, called Big Little Books. Never see them anymore though. Any way I think this book was about Terry and the Pirates. It was about a man that had been on a sail boat, taking a trip to China. His mingling with people, meeting with pirates on the way. and in China. It would show him eating large bowls of steaming hot rice with chop sticks, unheard of in my little country town in Michigan, Peacock, Michigan. A very fantastic story to a little boy like me, and especially with my Teddy Bear too. I talked to everyone who would listen about it, it fascinated me. Not knowing that I would go near there, to Japan to marry, raise a family, and to actually travel with my wife. From Okinawa to Taiwan, near China someday. But Teddy Bear and I took many imaginary trips there, imitating the book Terry and the Pirates. Fighting in our way, sailing on magic carpets. Sometimes driving our cars on ships, running bad guys out of the way scaring them over board. Riding our tricycle on board boats, mostly in the Chinese Junk style boats. Because those were the only pictures we had seen in the little book. But most of all we had just a very good time on our imaginary trip. I must say Trips to China, from Terry and the Pirates, Big Little Book.

We also ate a lot of imaginary large bowls of hot steaming rice with chop sticks. That we had only seen from pictures in Big Little Book. But Teddy Bear and I had fun, unforgettable fun.

Teddy Bear played games with my sister, brother and I. They were older, but they had no objection to my friend Teddy.

As did older adults, they understood. The years passed–and so did that part of life. I don't know what happed to my old friend.

After the teenage years came their demands etc. I was always a mechanical type person.

I became interested in automobiles removing, repairing engines, transmissions, cutting trees, railroad ties, things of that nature. Hauling coal, driving trucks etc. At age 17 entering the army, stayed for 25 years. Teddy Bear kind of got pushed back to the rear burner.

But is still there–warm in memories. My old Teddy Bear

Hi Teddy

My sister Willo May, Clarence and me

CANNING, TRACTORS, CELLARS ETC.

Throughout my traveling, having been to many places in the Far East. All across the USA watching people, their methods of transportation. I find it quite fascinating. Also the power used by farmers in their work especially farming. Because my young years were spent on a very small farm type setting. My father and mother always planted a little garden, in fact they used to use its products. My mother used to can the vegetables like green beans. There was also an item that looked like a watermelon, called a Citron, I think I've spelled it right. It was green, looked just like a watermelon, only was white with seeds and all inside. She would use the inside for cooking, because it wasn't sweet like a watermelon. Mother would sweeten it with sugar and make kind of a preserve with a flavoring or something added. She would also use this item for canning and keep it along with other canned items for winter table products. Canning was used by many people in days gone by, before many canned products could be found in stores like now. The folks then didn't put a lot of preservatives or seasoning in the items canned than would usually be done when the product was consumed. Except for the real sweet items, like apple preserves, citron preserves, things like that. The vegetable products were canned to be tasting almost, as they came from the field.

This canning was quite a procedure. A lot of jars were used usually quart size, some larger, some smaller I remember seeing mother use mostly quart size bottles. They were most of the time either labeled Ball or Mason jars, with a separate screw on lid. The bottle if it wasn't cracked or broken could be used over and over, kept for years and years of use. The tops had to be replaced each canning season. The lids or bottle tops I remember seeing two types the old type was a one piece lid. I believe it has glass piece inside the lid with a rubber ring for sealing, when screwed tight on the finished product. The other type which may still be used by people that still perform the old art of canning, Is a 2 piece lid that has a metal piece to fit on top of the bottle.

With a rubber ring on outer portion of the metal ring, to seal the product in the bottle. Then a round screw on cap is placed over the round metal piece and screwed down tight to seal the bottle until the canned product is ready for use.

These metal rings with rubber seal had to be purchased for use each canning season. The screw on portion of the sealing 2 piece type cap could be used over and over as long as it wasn't damaged or unserviceable.

Canning was quite an art, a lot of work too. The item to be canned whatever it might be had to be prepared Beans, corn, whatever had to be cleaned cooked then the bottles were placed in large containers clean, and boiled. Seemed everything had to be steaming hot, When all was ready the bottles would be filled with the desired product, and the lid screwed down tight. The process continued till bottles prepared were filled. Any left over's could be consumed next meal. Or if it was a sweet preserve product like apples, citron, peaches or such, by watching bright eyed children. The item usually was very delicious especially if a lot of hot biscuits, just might happen to be readily available, "with butter for the biscuit too".

After all these canned products cooled enough to handle they were at our place put in the cellar, which was a place my father constructed. My father was an old man, and he must have seen this type building in his younger days. I don't remember ever seeing another building of this type anywhere.

From what I can remember it must have been constructed in this manner because its size inside was about maybe 10ft. by 12ft. if that large, but it was always about that same temperature summer or winter. Even in winter nothing ever froze in there. Anyway back to the construction, the way I think it might have been made. Maybe a big hole must have been dug then a wall a ceiling made, I can't remember how the top or ceiling was made inside but it must have been very strong heavy material. The entire cellar was covered with sand, lots of sand, even grass grew on top. It looked like a little hill.

Looking at it now that I think about it when driving about west in areas where Native Americans live one can see constructions of that type. My father spent many years with folks of Indian culture and could speak some Indian Language quite well. Perhaps he learned of this type construction then. It was made separate from anything else and it was effective I can't remember of having to step down into it either. I'll take that back, maybe it had one big step down.

It had an entrance door, no windows. Had a shelf built to set the canned items on and bins to put items like apples and potatoes in. I remember the entrance door was set back with part of this roof sand over it.

Otherwise it was just a building called the cellar a little quiet building that stood, and stood, and stood there all while I grew to the age of 17 years, finished high school and left to spend 25 years in the army.

Another thing that always was of interest to me was tractors, even to this day they fascinate me especially the tracked type, like caterpillars. I like to see them in operation, when I was small there wasn't as many around like now, they are everywhere. Many made their own version of tractors, they would take off most of a vehicles body, and put truck differential's and transmissions in them. But they were never too successful. Sears or Montgomery Ward even sold a big wheel affair in their catalog that was adaptable to the model A Ford vehicle. I remember it was geared in a manner to be mounted so its gears would mesh with where the wheels were before removal, I think it worked. I think the cooling system was not too sufficient for heavy field work. But that era was interesting for a young mechanical minded young person with the auto age just budding, budding, budding all around and I was all eyes and ears.

Upon becoming a teenager I got my first auto a 1932 Ford Model B with model A engine in it. From there I was in the automotive field thru help from friends but mostly auto repair books and curiosity. I was pulling engines out of vehicles, overhauling them, and repairing transmissions, putting in clutches, the works Also worked in that field in the army for many years, till entering the electronics field. Still interested the old autos converted to wanna be tractors in my Michigan area of the world called Doodle-bugs. I never did make one, but always had a keen interest in them.

Several other little tractors came out about that time. I was attending an agricultural High school, and took several agricultural high school subjects. Heard other children that had farmer parents, talking about tractors they had.

Guess I took the subjects necessary, but decided I never wanted to be a farmer and was content to see, look and read about tractors, which I still do.

But I'm very happy to have had those experiences. They were just grand.

That was a nice era of time. I'll never forget it. It was necessary.

For now.

Place where I Albert Vicent was born. Peacock Mich. Aug. 31, 1929
Cellar is on right rear of the house, small hill structure.
Two leg standing device- right of the house near cellar, was used to hold and file
sharpen cross cut hand saws for wood cutting. Saw was placed upside down on
the stand to sharpen its teeth with a file. White on house top is snow.
Picture taken in Oct or Nov. 1952
House had been vacant for about 3 years, Mother moved to Baldwin, Michigan.

WORK AFTER AGE 42

The weather was nice in Monterey, CA. Of course it usually always is, As is the view there, in spots over the ocean Also the view when driving on highways that are located near the ocean. Like on the way to Big Sur where I like to camp- is simply breathtaking.

Having just returned from spending quite a few years in the Far East most of the time in Okinawa the view of the Ocean there is also lovely. But the climate is usually hot and humid. Because the little island is only about 60 miles long and 15 miles wide. So viewing the ocean is easily done most anytime one desires.

Also many other attractions, one especially is good clean air. Others lend themselves, to where one goes there, like the easy to get along with friendly people.

Arriving and to stay in Monterey County at the age of 42 after the family and I decided Michigan was too cold, was not a difficult decision to make. I worked at a car rental place for a few months then at a Firestone Tire Co. then at a Post Office. Didn't care for any of those places. A friend of mine had told me when I first retired from the military, to put in for a position with the school district. Which I had done but forgot about it. Well a position opened, I applied for the position and got it. It was a school Custodian, Believe it or not, I liked the job folks were nice, the hours were nice. I worked with the School District for 22 ½ years.

I worked and used my GI bill used it all, acquired my Associate of Arts degree. Also a Childhood Center Permit by taking a 2 year course in Early Childhood Education, a very interesting course. After I retired from the School District, happened to meet one of my Teachers at the Jr. College and she talked me into working 4 hours a day for the pre-school. I accepted the position and worked there 17½ years. I really enjoyed working with the children. There's always something new to do. A group of new different personalities, always.

It was interesting, must close now wife says its meal time again.

Have a good one.
Bye again.

Clarence, his wife, Haruko, Mother and Clarence's 1950 Ford

*Myself at, maybe,
Redstone Arsena
Govt. Housing Area.
Sometime around 1960*

40

Our house 2312, Tacoma Wash.
Haruko with the children
Nicky, Charley and Henry.

Our Place 2312,
S. Hosmer, Tacoma, Wash.
Children Nicky, Charley and Henry

COUNTRY EVENING SOUNDS

In the country where it's quiet right about twilight. When the sun sets and great long shadows, start to come from almost it seems-nowhere "(summer evenings)".

That's when the birds of night and others come out. Because that's the time they like. In Michigan where I lived, the Night Hawks start to play, they start to come alive it seems from rest by day. They climb high in the sky and dive down, you can hear them call as they swoop. Whooo-whoo-oo one will start. Then others join in, till the rhythm of the night is a sound of its own from over here-over there. Right here near, far away- then there, here and all over, in a way. This is of night in a blooming way, like noon follows morn of day.

Then the wip-poor-wills join in from near- then far away, far away then near. Then silence, silence complete, and a moon appears, climbs silent. While a coyote, and another answers and¼crickets chirp loud only crickets. With a tune unlike the call of a nighthawk- unlike the call of a whip-poor-will. But the call to another cricket who will understand, and will respond and must join in to sing. With the crickets in progress singing, and to thrill the dark of night with the cricket band, singing loud to and with the sounds of night. Then yet another group joins the night singing ribbit-ribbit-ribbit. The frogs, and they sing both loud and clear another sound in the night, beautifully loud and clear. But one can understand each singer participating in a night of singing heard in the quiet of country. Usually starting about Twilight when the sun sets.

It is most difficult, perhaps impossible to hear these night sounds in a large city where progress has covered these night singers homes, with concrete. Driving these choir participants far, far away-to where many are almost impossible or very hard to locate anymore. Even birds nests are a rare and protected rarity to find.

But progress is an important part of life and must be. I relish the fact of having once heard these sounds of the evening.

A special sound that was original, as the colors of a fully blossomed rainbow.

Haruko and I at our church playground.

ALLEN'S CHURCH

There was the old gravel road thru the middle of town, and the railroad ran right across it. Near Gales store, and a Squire Dingee Pickle Station was close to the railroad crossing too. The railroad crossing sign was about 8 or 10 feet tall an X type sign. One sign was on each side of the track, with beautiful green reflectors. About one inch in diameter, on each sign. Very tempting to small children with good throwing arms. Especially where good throwing material was as near as the stones under their feet on the gravel road where they stood. Occasionally a missing reflector appeared on the signs.

Allen's Church was also near the Pickle Station, and was an interesting building. Quite rustic in appearance, looked to be self made Which was a common practice in those days in the country. Because people didn't have much money, and if one could get the material folks built what they needed.

The old church was made mostly of railroad cross ties, the railroad very near was probably why. Older railroads were supported by wood crossties when they became worn, they were removed, new ties put in their place. The old ones were put in a neat stack near the railroad track. Where people would gather them and make buildings, fence posts, firewood, or whatever they desired. They weren't supposed to, but they did, no one seemed to stop them.

The old railroad ties were 8ft long usually of oak wood and quite heavy. Once taken to the location where they were to be used. A lot of times people would dig a long trench type hole. Maybe 2 or 3 feet deep. Stand them on end together for the walls. Fill the hole with sand, cut holes for windows, leave a space for doors finish the rest off with lumber and soon have a habitable, economical place. Many homes in Peacock, were made from railroad ties.

The bell tower to the old church was very rough looking, with boards not nailed straight. It was maybe about 20 or 25 feet high, with a bell mounted in it. The bell was mounted in a separate metal frame with a large wheel on one side, with a rope tied to the wheel. That extended to floor level, and when the rope was pulled. The bell would swing back and forth in its metal frame and the clapper a piece of metal round shaped like a ball with about a 6 or 8 inch stem on it. Fastened so it could swing back and forth hitting the bell as the rope was pulled making the bell ring. The bell though sounded very nice across the open Peacock, Michigan country side.

I can remember when I was quite young maybe about 9 years old. While walking into the church one evening, I felt the wind of something's whiz past the rear of my head and shoulders, hitting the ground behind me. It was the clapper that had fell from the bell. It makes me almost shudder even today, a few more months I'll be 80 years of age, If that about 5 pounds of metal would have struck me on top of the head from its about 25 ft height in the tower what might have happened.

I guess the creator must have been saving me for other things in life and I appreciate that, I really do.

Inside the church were old used long straight back wood and iron folding school benches and straight back chairs. Each bench was about 10 feet long. The church had a poured concrete floor an old foot pumped organ for music and a handmade podium for the minister.

Mr. Allen lived on about a 1 or 2 acre piece of land with his wife. Two grandchildren, and a mean dog named Thunder. I remember he raised strawberries. Sometimes he would bring them to church, and make strawberry ice cream in a hand cranked freezer. We children could take turns cranking it, till the ice cream inside. Got real hard to turn then everyone could eat the ice cream. and scrape ice cream from the dasher. Inside the can that mixed the ice cream when the handle was turned. The Ice cream tasted really good too.

I can remember many songs and things we learned at the old church. Also Mr. Allen driving his old about 1924 Buick car. I really don't know if Mr. Allen really built the old church or not, but everybody called it Allen's Church. Peacock Michigan is a very small place, maybe about 40 people lived there. There still isn't much in peacock. All of the old past that I knew, grew up with, is gone.

But when I think of the past, seems there's a faint whistle from a steam locomotive coming, maybe leaving Peacock. Oh, say-I think I hear the old church bell ringing, no it's voices, young voices, that must be the children playing at Peacock School. But looks like there's a mist covering things, maybe that's not mist it's probably dust from a car passing by on the gravel road. You know how those young folks drive those new fangled cars. Why they go 35, 40, almost 50 miles an hour. They almost fly.

The old Allen's Church, the school house, most of the folks, are gone.

But when the wind whistles around a building like an approaching old steam locomotive it's a reminder, that, the past is a step in direction of the present, also the future and, Bye.

Allen's Church
My sister Willo Mae Vicent

AN EXPERIENCE

The old Redman place was about 4 or 5 miles from our place. My Brother-in-law's father came by one day, and asked me, Think I was maybe 12 or 13, maybe about 14 years old.

Albert my horses are over at the Red man place will you go get them. You can take this halter it's easy to put on. Ride bareback he told me which horse to ride bareback, and lead the other he will follow. They are workhorses, want to do that for me Albert? I'll pay you. Think he gave me 2 or 3 dollars.

I thought about it a little bit having never done anything like that before. Seen a lot of people doing that riding horses, hitching wagons etc. Ok Albert, he repeated. It was kind of a lazy day. Wasn't doing anything special anyway. Also, thought it might be, kind of exciting riding a horse that far.

So, off I went, it was a good walk, found the horses, put on the halter. It was easy, just put the bridle that the piece that goes in the horse's mouth. Slip the rest of the halter over the horses head to down over the horses head. Throw the reins over the horses head to down over the horses neck. Hop on, use the reins to pull the horses head left or right, the directions you want to go, and away you go.

I had a little trouble getting on, not being a trained rider. Because the horse is quite high for a short guy not used to hanging on to an animal, swinging his body that high. But the horse was surprisingly understanding, and stood still, helping me get on its back. Once I got on, stretching ones legs all the way across a horses back is quite far. Kind of pulls you apart at first but you get used to it. The horses backbone kind of bumps you a little at first. riding bareback (no saddle), but the horse is warm, with a horsey smell.

Anyway we bumped along down the country road the other horse followed. Even trotted a little bit once or twice. The old horse would stop sometime nibble a little grass, or pull a leaf off a tree we passed as we went along. Didn't seem to pay much attention to my commands to stop doing that. Maybe the horse thought this guy's no cowboy. Which I wasn't but we made it back ok. It was truly an experience. The horse kind of gave me an interesting look as I took the halter off of its head.

That was years ago, but for some reason I always remember it. I also remember a little about hitching a horse to a wagon. I remember you throw the harness over the horses back (of course you have to put the halter on horses head the bridle in its mouth hook up the reins to guide the horse). After the harness is put on, the horse is backed up to the wagon the two poles one on each side of the horse is hooked to the harness. The chains to the single tree to pull the wagon is hooked up and the harness secured to the horse. Reins are thrown back to the wagon, climb in to the wagon seat give the horse command gid-yup and away you go. If I remember gee is to the right. Haw is to the left. Pull back to stop the horse. These are rein commands. By pulling the reins giving these commands, the horse is to respond turning left, right, or stopping. On the wagon the poles or tongue of the wagon that the horse was backed into, was to turn the wagon left or right, when the horse is given those commands.

Horses are interesting animals and served much in settling. This and several countries and places around the world. Still there are many horses.

Brother-Clarence Vicent, Mother-Edna May Vicent, Father-William Vicent, Dog-Skippy and another dog.

House where I was born.
Peacock, Michigan
Picture taken maybe 1944-45
My Father made the house.

KEROSENE LIGHTS, WOOD AND COAL STOVES

In the summer, in the dark, you could hear the crickets chirping, their music was nice. Nothing else ever sounded the same, and if you were quiet really, really, really quiet. The crickets would chirp louder, and louder, and louder. Till their chirp seemed one cricket chirping continuously right after another, one after the other without stopping. Like one large, very large cricket choir, it was just awesome.

Also with the crickets choir usually in the country, dark colored frogs could be heard. Croaking, making their sounds, nightly sounds, and way off in distance, a coyote's call.

Fireflies too would always appear, and light the night with their lights. Turning them off and on like little sparklers, along with the crickets and frogs. Evening in the summer in real dark void of lights, is an experience a beautiful, experience.

Of course in the winter its different no crickets, fireflies, frogs. But coyotes are there and on a moonlit night when one can view the heavens. With soft snow gently quiet falling, falling down. It appears to be soft ever so soft specks of nether, visible yet falling. Gently, touching, damp like, piling, falling to the ground.

In Peacock Michigan there were no lights at night, people used kerosene lamps. A lamp with a wick made of web type cloth material, with one end in a reservoir of kerosene. The other end of the wick, extending thru an adjustable device. Controlled by a little knob that could be turned, raising and lowering the wick. When more wick was turned up clockwise, the flame on the oily wick burned bright. If turned counter clockwise, the flame would be low.

The device that held the wick, also supported the glass globe, that surrounded the wick. The glass globe, called the chimney, gave the flame more brilliance. To light a room, a home or any place one was using a kerosene lamp. There were also lanterns of this type, for outdoors use, that worked the same way. These were made of metal, with a carrying handle type of kerosene light. They all worked much in the same manner. These type lights is what my mother and father used, to light our home. I done my school work by it, my mother would turn it down low at night. Leaving it burning all night to light the house, She usually waited up till we growing children, got safely home. When we started driving autos going our different ways, and coming home late in the evening. Going off to town about 10 or 12 miles distant to see our friends.

I can almost hear mother or father now saying "that you Albert". My father would say, "Everything ok", and my parents would then drift off to sleep. First tho, usually telling me "there's some food in the warmer". That was a compartment over the old kitchen wood burning cook stove, that kept items warm for quite some time. From the wood burning cook stove that usually had 4 cooking rings, over the cooking area. That could be removed to put wood or coal in (a front door), for fuel for the fire. If the draft for air for the fire was closed or opened, the fire would burn high or low. Naturally then, the fuel would be consumed more quickly or slowly. Keeping the food in the warmer for longer periods of time. There was also an oven, to bake things on the cook stove. That usually worked pretty good.

Also the heating stove for heating the home worked much in the same manner. Only it was used for heating, constructed in a different style, but worked in the same manner. Burned wood or coal, heated the room it was in, with the help of the cooking stove. Homes were kept fairly warm, till the fire went out. Then in the winter things got cold, real cold in the Michigan winters. Ice would be on the drinking water buckets, sometimes 2 or 3 inches thick.

My father usually started the fire early to warm the house. When we got up it would be cold, but we were used to that. Folks used inside commode for toilets that were emptied in the mornings. Everybody did that. There were outside toilets, no inside plumbing. Especially in the country and in Peacock Michigan. But we survived.

Peacocks still there with about maybe now, 40 or 50 people. Good old Peacock Michi- gan. My home town. The summers still have crickets, firefly's light, frog's evening's sounds, and displays. Now there are electric lights, I don't know about the city sewage there. I doubt that luxury is there yet. Folks probably use septic tanks.

My wife Haruko Vicent

This picture, has been inspirational, in Creating, and also during our marriage.

Through the Korean War years was with me many ways.

Through the years, and still is one of my favorite pictures

.1948 to now 9/27/2009
And always will be.

HOW I MET MY WIFE

The ship slid silent into Yokohama Harbor

As¼¼.

We watched the small boats moving there men with strange looking footwear that looked more like gloves on their feet, yet they moved very agile on the boats. We later learned the strange footwear seen was called Ta-Bel in Japan and used with great success there over the years.

This was in the year of 1948 month of January, I was in military and was to be in Yokohama for about 2 years. Being very young, about 18, my impression was wow, what a place. What is this, indeed interesting and looked different much different from the deck of a ship too. Though, I did notice a Coca-Cola sign displayed near a building.

We later, after the ship docked, went thru a replacement depot and were assigned to the place we would go. My place to be was in Yokohama Japan. The street car ran right in front of the camp which made it very convenient when going on pass, to catch the street car and go places.

I later bought a bicycle. It was used, very used, but I had it repaired at a bicycle shop. There were many of them everywhere, because at that time not many autos, were in use. There were some 3 wheel truck type vehicles. With a little box on back to haul things, some buses, some taxi's. Most buses and taxies then ran off charcoal, for fuel, a fire burned on the rear of the vehicle. With a long tube running over the top of the vehicle to the engine. Carrying the combustible product, through and to, the engine.

I used my bicycle a lot, I was young, and there were a lot of local people using bicycles too. So when I had time off, away on my bicycle I went, folks were nice to me and I was in turn nice to them. I learned enough of the language to be understood, and this helped at that time but no more. The military at that time was still segregated, there were African and Caucasian units, mine was African. Some people were curious but not much, after they get to know us, as we them. Lots of the local people worked on the military establishments, very soon trust was established. That thru the years that has followed, has proven to be great. The people were not tall, neither was I, so right away I kind of found places, friends of my choice. Where I could fit in. Got a fondness for the area that still exists today, 61 years later.

After being there a few months I met a young lady though she was 8 years older than I. We got along all right. Also met her family, they accepted me, were very nice people, still are 61 years later. We visit Japan quite often, they too have visited my family here. In fact my wife's mother came to visit for a 6 month visit and stayed for 18 years.

To get back to our acquaintance, and later marriage in the military after my first coming to Japan, when my tour was up I had came back to America. We had not married in fact had not considered it. But after my return, love is strong, indeed strong. I wanted to return some- way and did, though I had to go thru the Korean War to do it. While there I was hospitalized for a while, sent to Japan to a hospital in Kobe where I stayed for a few months. There I sent for my later to be wife, we met again, discussed if marriage should be. Decided it should be, and¼. started the paper work, which was lengthy to accomplish. The military made it that way which I think was good. Because if you really did not want to go through with the matter, you would get discouraged and stop.

My case was extremely difficult because I was in the war zone of Korea, the would be wife in Japan. And I was moving all over in Korea. Sending papers back and forth to Japan, going to Chaplin interviews Who was trying to discourage me, but¼they finally gave up, and permitted our marriage. I took a 2 week R&R (rest and recuperation) leave to Japan in November 1951. To start our life and marriage which will be 58 years in Nov. this year. Good Lord willing. Three children, 6 grandchildren and 4 great grandchildren later.

I brought my wife to America in 1952 we landed in Seattle Washington by ship from Yokohama. Got off the ship with her silver aluminum suitcase with her belongings and my military gear in a duffle bag. And nothing more except God's blessings which has been good, very good.

During the years of military we traveled quite a lot. California to Alaska, State of Washington, New Jersey, Tacoma Washington, Okinawa Japan. Maryland, Korea, California (discharge retirement) in 1972, and California for the last 35 years.

There has been sunshine, clouds storms, rainbows too. But mostly sunshine and rainbows, on the way, so far ¼. On the way thru. Hey, thanks Creator and Creation.

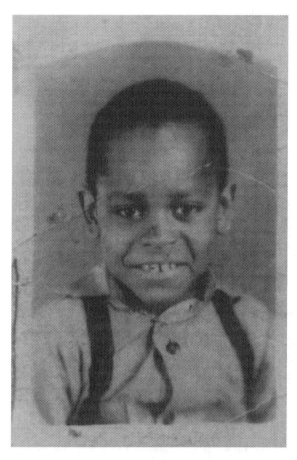

My only boyhood picture.
When I was maybe 7 or 8
years of age.
Not many folks had cameras then.
My family had none.
Maybe picture made about
1935-36-37

BEE STINGS

There wasn't many cars, and most of the cars had wheels that were pretty high. I guess to travel on the country roads, which usually composed of 2 path type trails. Of one width, made by wagons usually pulled by horses or oxen. The automobiles were of about the same width, so they fit and traveled on these trails. Till better highways were built and automobiles were made lower for greater speeds. These type of roads went to many country homes, farms, stores and other places.

Of course there were steam trains on railroads. My family when I was a small child did not have an automobile. We lived in a home that was serviced by wagon type roads for a while. Also had a piece of ground located far out in the country, which the train at one time serviced. But the rails had been removed, and the train service was no longer there. So we walked to this little piece of ground, where my parents done a little farming. Raised corn, beans, pumpkins, squash, etc.

We didn't have an automobile, so my father made a little cart with 2 wheels and handle in front to pull it. With the wheels about 3 ft. in diameter, with wooden spokes, metal rims, around the wood like a wagon wheel no rubber tires. But it worked quite well on the trail type roads where it was used. The box was maybe 4 or 5 ft. long and about 3 ft. wide with someone pulling, others pushing, something could be transported. And this is what we used for hauling light items, with larger items. We had to find a neighbor with a horse and wagon, or someone with an automobile and trailer, or a truck. Which not too many folks had.

The place where this gardening spot was located was about 2 miles from our house. Every time we went to tend to the farmer type work, we would load the necessary items on the little cart. Hoes, shovels, mattock, and other items necessary, especially water to drink. Now this is the item that was kept cool then, in a much different manner than today. Where a thermos type container is used.

My father used an old system, Natures system. He would fill a little jug, I remember, made of a crock type material about ½ in. thick. Kind of mixed brown and white in color, with about a 1 ¼ in. opening at the top where a cork was inserted, but his bottle had no cork. The cork had been replaced with a whittled wood stopper. My father was very handy at whittling and liked to work with wood, with his Barlow pocket knife. The system used to keep this jug of water cool was this: My father would dig a hole in ground in a shady spot, and dig where the ground was nice damp and cool. Place the bottle in this hole, put brush leaves or anything around it. This would keep the water pretty cool for quite a while. If you wanted water you could come drink.

The system was good except little people, like I was at the time. Who liked to play more than really work, and still wanted a drink. Got the area where the water was buried mixed and removed covering from a yellow jacket bee nest. They immediately came out of their hole in the ground and stung me severely. All over the arms, the neck, hands, head, face area any place they could find to land. They were very unhappy.

My father, I think my brother was there too, they came to my rescue. Because I was letting the entire wooded area know about the bees attack. I had the body scream and cry EQ turned on full blast, because that hurt. My father and brother swooshed the bees away with their arms and hats or whatever. Or maybe the bees felt they had made me suffer enough, and just left. I know the buzzing and stinging stopped.

My father didn't seem to get excited, he just took it all in stride, and told me, "Lad, just be quiet and take it easy. You'll be ok." He watched me. He smoked an old corn cob pipe, and used good old summer time smoking tobacco. I remember seeing him put a whole bunch of it in his mouth chew it remove it and put it over the bee stings. Then he pointed out where the water jug was, told me to get my drink and go sit in the shade till he got things together. So we could load things on the cart, and we walked back home.

Those yellow jacket bees stung me quite bad, the stings swelled but not real bad. I don't remember getting sick from it. It's an incident in my life, I'll always remember though. I think then, maybe I was 7 or 8 yrs. old.

That piece of ground was, if I can remember, was 11 acres in size. Lots of trees on it with about ¾ or maybe 1 acre cleared for a house and gardening. It was close to where a railroad used to be, an area still known as the old grade. Lots of animals live in the area. My father used to complain when he done his gardening. That in spite of his fence, when corn and garden items were young, and growing, the deer with great ease. Would jump the fence eat their fill and with great ease exit or jump over the fence, and out. He knew because they left their tracks on most of his garden.

I wish I had pictures of that era of life, but not many had cameras. I know we didn't and in spite of the missing pictures. Peacock with history, is preserved quite ok, for today, in a very special way.

Our house was across the gravel road directly in front of this school house about maybe only 200 or 300 yards between the buildings. My wife and mother standing in front of the school, when Haruko first came to America, 1952.

Mother, Fred Douglas and Haruko
At his store (the old Comstocks Store)
In Peacock, Michigan
Taken same day as the picture in front of the school.

PEACOCK SCHOOL

Near Gales store there was the old train depot it was just down the track. Where the railroad crossed over the old gravel road that ran right thru the middle of Peacock. That was a little town in Michigan.

Then there was Allen's Church, and not far from it was the old Peacock school. A one room school house, with a long wood coal shed in the back, attached to the schoolhouse. The school used a large wood and coal stove for heating.

There were always farm animal around the school, because people let their animals run loose at that time they would gather them in the evenings for milking and house them. In day the animals just wandered around, eating grass, some time breaking someone's fence. Eating folks growing green items, then an explanation by the owner was necessary. But no one paid attention to the animals, they ranged all over the town. Students could usually look out the schoolhouse windows and see cows. People had to be wary of droppings cow pies, etc. They were usually around somewhere.

The old Peacockthschool being only one room had grades from kindergathrten thru 8th grade and sometimes 9 and 10th graders. But usually was kindergarten thru 8 grade. The student desks were made of wood and iron with folding seats and desks to hold books. With a well (large hole) to hold ink, a lot of writing was with a wood handled pin. With a metal point that could be dipped in the ink well for writing. The ink well was also sometime used to dip girls sitting in front of boys with lengthy hair for a hair dip by the boys. If caught by the girls they usually got well scolded, even slapped, or made into a boyfriend.

There was a hand pump in front of the school where larger boys or girls pumped the water. To fill and replace water in the push button gravity type drinking fountain. The water in the water bucket with the turn by screwing in or out spicket to drain water from. To wash hands with, sit there also, on a little shelf.

There was an inside restroom at the rear of the school, left side for girls, right side for boys. Restrooms had a large tank at bottom where water was poured daily. The restrooms were pumped by a visiting truck when necessary. There was also an outside toilet sometimes turned over on Halloween night, as was the rope pulled bell on top of the school. By mischievous larger school boysndor Halloween spirits. No one ever told who did it.

There was also 2 story to the school, that was known as the town hall. It was used for elections and for our school functions. Such as Christmas Programs, preparation for the programs and other town functions. When something was held in the town hall over the school it was quite a big deal in Peacock. Because that was the hall in our town of only about 40 people. When it got dark in Peacock with no electricity, and only kerosene lights. It got dark and the town hall lights at night, was something big, real big.

When Election Day came, outside the school was active. People were voting. There were a lot of horses and wagons, not many folks had cars. The ones that came were quite old but modern then. Like model T Fords, Old Star's, Essex, Dodge Brothers, some Model A fords etc. Lots of people cranked their cars by hand to start them. We children would accept, watch, and marvel at their dexterity and often anger. When the vehicle wouldn't start.

The teacher would caution us to watch out and be careful. During town hall functions and play on opposite sides of the building, as much as possible. During those times with no playing of one of our favorite games which was Anti-I-Over. Throwing the ball over the schoolhouse one side to the other. If caught when it came over the catcher would shout and come running around to try to tag someone, who would then repeat the process. One never knew which side of the building the catcher would arrive from, Of course that kept the gameinteresting. Small or not too strong armed students had to be careful not to break windows. Some windows were broken on the upper floor mostly. Peacock was quite a school. Lots of memories.

It was closed about 1941 or 1942, not enough children. The students were sent to Dickson High Scthool in Brethren Michigan about 30 miles away. Where grades were from kinder-garten to 12 grade. I was in the 6th grade then, and graduated from Dickson High School in Brethren Michigan, May 1947.

But I will always remember both schools, created lots of memories there.

TREES, RAILROAD TIES, ETC. AND HAULING COAL

The place we were going was only about 5 miles from our place. We were going there to work, and were going there to see how the work was to be performed.

Having helped our father and watched him cut down trees, we knew quite a lot about the tree cutting process. But had to find out how to cut down the trees, and cut them into oak tree railroad tie length, Also poplar tree bolt length, for paper manufacture. It did not take long to find out what was expected, to do the work. It was hard work, strict manual labor.

My brother, I think had just finished high school and I was maybe 14 years old. I could only do this on school or summer vacation time, sometimes on weekends. When we cut trees then it was all by hand power. There were no chainsaws at that time. It was all use of an ax to cut the undergrowth or brush, to get to the tree trunk and undercut the tree. That is to determine which way the tree leans, and direction wind is blowing, to aid the tree in falling. So it won't pinch the saw.

Our saws used then were a crosscut type. One person on each end of the saw, one person pulled the saw one way, then released pressure on the saw, held it against the tree to cut the tree. The process repeats itself. Each person pulls, releases, pulls, releases the saw until the tree is cut down. An undercut is performed to prevent splitting of the tree when it falls.

A tree cutter looks at a tree determines which way the tree leans. Then determines the depth of the undercut needed, then hand saw, to cross-cut saw the tree to depth, of the under- cut. Use an axe to chop a slant cut to the saw under cut, on the tree. Go around on the side of the tree opposite the undercut and proceed with the saw, to cut down the tree. If the undercut is of proper depth, when the tree is cut and falls. It won't split from the undercut side up the tree trunk, when it starts to fall. There should be a clear break between the tree and the tree stump.

The tree cutter always calls with a loud voice so all can hear TIMBER when the tree starts to fall so if anyone is near they can clear the area, Because a large tree is heavy, and can kill, squash, a person like an ant.

Once the tree hits the ground we had to get busy trim it, cut the limbs off and cut it into 8 ft. lengths. If I remember correctly, not under 10 inch. in diameter for railroad ties, which we got 25¢ each for an 8 ft, piece. It took a long time to make much money. A good day one might make 6 or 8 dollars that was spending money, for a school kid. Hard work though. Hot in summer and I can remember in winter, wading through snow almost waist high, because there are no paths where trees are.

The trees when they are cut in 8 ft. lengths, are still round because the tree is round. They are loaded on a truck and taken to a saw mill where the 4 sides are cut into slab making wood, from each side. Then a square railroad tie is produced. The railroad ties were cut from Michigan white oak trees. The poplar bolts we cut in 8ft. lengths also. I think we got 25¢ each for them also. I don't know how they were processed to paper though, I can remember cutting them.

After I got my driver's license there was a grocery store, in the little town of Baldwin. About 12 miles from Peacock, that sold coal for heating. The coal would come in on railroad cars, my brother and I were paid 90¢ an hour, To unload the cars and haul the coal, to the stores storage area. Then deliver it, as the store owner sold it to people.

I was driving the trucks, loading them too, at 15 years old, with about 2 tons or more of coal. Delivering it putting snow chains on dual tires, making my spending change at quite a young age. During weekends, vacation time etc, also working on old cars. Always or most always earning enough by spreading the change thoughtfully, and with care. To take care of teenager needs with sweat, and honest earned change.

Learned a lot which has never been forgotten or regretted over the years.

I'm bottom row, 2ⁿᵈ from the left.
Picture was made in Alaska, Ladd Air Force Base. Fairbanks, Alaska
June 25, 1955

A 12 MILE WALK

When I had finished my Army base training and had taken our 20 mile hike with full backpack and came home on furlough was the only time I can remember of doing it. This was walking the 12 miles from the town of Baldwin in Michigan to Peacock, where we at that time lived. I had rode I think with my brother to Baldwin, to visit with some friends I knew. Before joining the army and stayed there all day, and didn't want to come home with my brother, and told him I would find a way home. He wanted me to come with him because Peacock and Baldwin are both quite small, Peacock about 40 people, Baldwin at that time maybe 6 or 800 people. We are speaking of a distance of 12 miles and there transportation just doesn't exist. My brother and I both knew this. So I planned to walk the distance, and was thinking in my mind about the 20 mile hike I had recently had in the army was 18 yrs old then. Thought I owned the world, and the 12 miles seemed no problem.

So I stayed in town, till late, visiting and walked home. The 12 miles wasn't a problem. I'll never forget it though. The night was with occasional light snow, moonlight but cloudy. Very, very quiet, because there were almost no cars that traveled that highway. Then almost anytime especially, not at almost midnight. I don't think I encountered any automobiles. It was a nice walk, very, very quiet. As the snowflakes fell I could almost hear them. When I looked at the clouds shrouded moon of the night sky, the snowflakes were like so many little dark spots, falling from the sky. Only the many country trees surrounded me, as I plodded, walking with youthful steps of a then 18 year old-on, and on the snow crunching beneath my combat boots. Because I was dressed in my army uniform, it was comfortable, nice to walk in. Hands and feet warm, from the walk.

When the furlough was finished, I was to be going, by train to California. My basic training was completed, had been trained. In the kind of work I was to do, and was going overseas to a new place, a new country. The lengthy World War II was finished, being very young, something I could feel was being awakened in me. "Travel", I later found I loved to, witness new places, see new things, see how other folks do things we do. Different strokes, effective, most times very effective. At the time I didn't know it but I was on the eve of my new career, where I would remain for the next 25 years. Meeting my wife, raising a family, taking them with me, most places, traveling, having good, bad times. As most people (they make you mature, help you grow) was to experience many wonderful things. I didn't realize that at that time, that understanding came later. As the moments, hours, years, continue in silence, with silence to miraculously unfold.

I could and did feel a new beginning, a new experience was happening. As I walked the 12 miles from Baldwin to Peacock that evening, by myself, through the country woods. Where, bear, deer, wolves, coyotes, many animals live, which I never seen that evening. Perhaps they seen me and wondered what's he doing out here so late by himself, just walking. Let's go get him. But maybe their friends said, "Aw, he's too small". At that time I only weighed about maybe 140 pounds, and I'm glad they felt that way too. If they would have chased we would have ran fast, pushed a lot of snowflakes all the way to thru and perhaps past Peacock. Because I wouldn't have missed the then approaching next 25 years for nothing, they were great.

I completed the walk that evening to Peacock, which was a very quiet little country, very country town. Of about 40 people, that I could see as I walked past the old Allen's place, down past Jones Place. Turned at Sharp's place, down past the little store, that had been closed for years. Across the old railroad tracks, down past Allen's Church. Kept walking and there was my house, with a kerosene light turned down low. Like mother always done, waiting for we children to return.

I remember I stood and looked at the scene for awhile, something one doesn't see from a distance that I can't remember witnessing since, after walking that distance to a country home. A little house sitting with snow softly falling in country quiet all around. A lot went through my mind those few seconds of long ago much of which their memory remains. (Though the house, father, mother, are no longer having passed with passing years). Oh yes, now back to the completion of the now memorable 12 mile walk from where I could view the low burning kerosene lamp which my mother had kept on for my return which I could view for quite a distance.

It took me maybe 5 minutes to walk to the old white school house which our house was directly in front of and thru the open gateway to our front door. Which I opened and walked in, and mother said as I was opening the door, "That you Albert", "Yes it's me", "There's something in the warmer for you if you're hungry", "Ok mother I'll check" and my brother who had come home earlier said "I believed you, you ok Albert? How did you get here?" Told him "I walked." "All the way from

Baldwin?" I replied "Yes of course, I came down past Allen's place", "That way that's thru the woods" he said. I told him "Aw, nothing was there, not even a squirrel."

Think I ate some baked beans mother had prepared, and consumed some deep crusted apple cobbler mother had prepared and left in the warmer. The warmer is a compartment that keeps items warm in a sliding door compartment over old wood cook stoves. Done a pretty good job too. As long as the fire remained burning. After I had my little home cooked left over's with mothers love early morning meal. I went to sleep in my own old high school bed and slept very good. In quiet old Peacock Michigan.

Thru memory is a good way to travel and it don't cost much. There's no one to check your baggage or ticket you go free and come or go back any time. Seems everybody, everything is still there like you left it (except you). I wonder if everything will always stay that way maybe, we'll never really know. Bye, Al

Clarence, Ernest Thomas, his wife and his model A Ford Truck.

Ernest Thomas, his catipillar and me

Clarence, Ernest Thomas, his wife and his model A Ford Truck.

Ernest Thomas, his catipillar and me

2 WHEEL BICYCLE

Winters were cold in Mich. but spring had a way of making one forget the cold, anyway there was lots of good things to do in the winter, interesting things too. Like downhill sledding you would pull the sled uphill and slide downhill. Then walk back up hill and repeat slide down again. Some hills were better, they had a better slope and not too hard to climb either or you would get tired early and have to go home. One thing I had at home that I really liked was not a tricycle because it had no pedals. It was not a 2 wheeler because it had 3 wheels but I could sit on it, put my feet on the floor, and push myself all over the house. That was fun. It also had a bell on it. I was really little, small I guess for sledding but sledding was fun, and I tagged along anyway because my older brother and his friends was there. Even though they wasn't very happy with the task, they watched out for me pretty good.

One of my request to older people my parents and older children too, was; I want a 2 wheel bicycle very soon because my brother had one and I wanted one. I seen pictures of them in the country folks wish book, the Sears catalog, and when I felt like it, I let folks know my desire. Bicycles cost money and money was not something my family had a lot of. So my request was put on the back burner, by all except my brother's friend, my friend too. We called him "Bud" nickname for his name Ernest Thomas. He didn't talk about it but kept it in his memory. He was a very mechanical gifted person, his father had the only garage in town, the Thomas Garage, he didn't get much business other than his own mechanical work because there just wasn't many cars around then, but he had lots of mechanical things of his own like a caterpillar, a threshing machine, car, motorcycle and things. So Bud had a lot of mechanical expertise. Bud had a sister but no brother. So one day in the spring Bud came to our place one morning I believe it was about the month of April or May with a 2 wheel bicycle. I believe it had about 20 or 24 inch wheels on it he had put a lot of old bicycle parts, together and made a bicycle.

He made the announcement "Albert I fixed a bicycle for you". I was so happy. I still remember that bicycle my mother came to look at it, my father, sister, brother, all the family. I think even the dog and cat seeing all the commotion came, and checked what was in progress too.

My parents asked Bud the price of the bicycle. I think Bud replied nothing. Anyway the price I remember being settled on was one dollar. My father told me "Lad" (he was an older man age 80 when I was born, he always called us lads.) and he said "Lad, you help pay for the bike." So I broke my piggy bank open, I think it was an old Hershey cocoa can or Karo syrup can, and took out some coins, my parents put in the rest, and paid Bud. He was happy I was overjoyed. My first and very own bicycle.

Now about the bicycle, it needed something to make it really roadworthy. Like tires because the front tire was filled with sawdust. Which was plentiful in those days, because the stores used blocks of ice cut in winter from lakes. Stored between layers of sawdust kept in outdoor sheds, dug out in summer, to sell. To folks that had ice boxes to store eating items in, like refrigerators now. So the front tire had sawdust, I think the rear tire held air. We later got a tire, painted the bicycle with a paint brush. There was no spray cans of paint then, made some other minor repairs. I used the old bike for a long time. It was my pride and joy. My very first 2 wheeler.

My brother and I and our wives visited with Ernest and his family a few years ago. We again discussed the old bicycle and old times. Bud was aged in his 70's then. Bicycles fill a part of child and adulthood. My first 2 wheel bicycle was very special to me. I'll always remember it. That bicycle, friends and I had much fun together.

Gales Store with ice house

Allen's Church in Peacock, Michigan.
My sister, Willo Mae Vicent

Old Steam Engine Train
Streamline Train

With Haruko, Charley, Henry myself, Haruko's mother and Hei Jiro's first wife.
At a train station in Tokyo or Osaka, Japan

PEACOCK STORES

An old gravel road went right through the middle of town down past the ranger station. It was quite busy when the CCC Camp, Camp Axton was there. I believe that was how it was spelled. The old road went on down past Mr. Drureys house, past the road to the African Americans cemetery. Which was about an acre of land given by a lady to African Americans because back in the 1920's segregation was still alive and well. The little cemetery was used, I think about 20 people are buried there now. My brother showed me the grave of one Caucasian man buried there, his grave is about in the middle of the cemetery. About 30 or 40 feet away from African American sites, suggesting a belief even in death exists. If one continued on the old road a mile and half more and would it would lead to Baldwin Mich, about 12 miles from Peacock. There were about 40 people living in Peacock in the 1930's, no electric or running water in the town. But folks learned to accept Peacock the way as it was, and raised good families.

The little town only had 2 stores there was Gales Store, it was right near the railroad track where the railroad track crossed the gravel road. Which was about a city block away. Gales store had a nice piece of concrete in front maybe 30 ft. by 10 ft. with a porch roof over it. That was nice to stand under, and ride my tricycle on. Because Peacock didn't have any sidewalks or concrete except when county garage was made. It was about 150 or 200 ft. across the old gravel road from Gales store. Or between the store and the railroad grade that was an old logging railroad that ran by Peacock years before my time. For some reason there was a trench on each side of it with a raised portion in the middle where the old trains ran. The area got called the old grade. Anyway, the county garage that was built in the mid 1930's had a concrete slab about maybe 40 ft. by 25 ft. in front of it. The building was used to store equipment in, and children would ride bicycles, on the nice slab of concrete. It had room to ride a 2 wheeler on especially if you were learning to ride and were careful. When someone holding the bike let go and you wobbled went straight for awhile while trying to turn in a big circle on the concrete slab. You had to learn with no training wheels then. I can't remember seeing any training wheels at that time. No band aids either, for skinned knees.

Our little town only sported 2 concrete slabs in town, the rest of the hard area to ride bicycles and walk on was the old gravel road. That got kind of a hard surface after cars ran over it for a long time. You could walk with care or ride a bicycle on the road carefully watching out for cars, there weren't a whole lot of them, but one had to be careful. You could usually see or hear a car coming from a distance. Especially if it had not rained for a while, there would be a big cloud of dust. When it passed and the dust cloud followed, that smelled of gas and dust vapor. An old car would pass by, it would probably be going about maybe 30 to 40 miles per hour. Old Model T Fords and others of that era didn't go too much over 45 or 50 miles per hour. Cruising and being on gravel roads with bumps chuck holes etc. hindered top speeds severely. But people managed and got around. Kicked up some dust, passing by.

Inside Gales store one could find a big glass case on a counter with candy, my favorite was, and I really used to like them too, they were dome shaped pieces of candy. Round on the base and tapered toward the top, where they were smooth and rounded. With white sweet substance inside. Outside each piece was covered with sweet brown chocolate, boy they were good. I think one could get 3 or 5 pieces for a penny.

Once in a while we kids would splurge, when we could find enough empty soft drink bottles. You could get 2¢ for a soda bottle and 5¢ for a milk bottle. People used to go to a store and buy Coca Cola or other soft drinks. From a large cooler with large ice hunks and water to keep the drink cool. Then they would drive off drinking the drink, and throw away the bottles on the road side, We children would look for them, take them to the store and redeem them for whatever we could get. Sometimes we could even afford a large 5¢ butterfinger, milkyway, or three musketeers candy bar, when they started making them, I think it was in late 1930's or early 1940's, along came the Snicker Bar. It was also good, of course there were also other brands, but I remember those brands for some reason Maybe they were at front of the candy case.

Gales store also had some canned goods. Canned goods wasn't real big like now. Guess there has been more advanced methods to preserve canned items over the years. There were a lot of salted items then, like salt bacon etc. Fresh meat was usually kept in a large ice cooled cooler Where lunch meats, ring baloney, hot dogs, hamburgers, were kept. Then there were household items like a few brooms, dust pans etc. In the store.

Comstocks store was right down the street about 200 ft. away. It was maybe a little larger with much of the same items.

Both stores sold gasoline. No, maybe only Comstocks store sold gasoline. I remember it had the old hand operated pump. You pumped gasoline up with a hand operated pump, with a handle. That you pushed from left to right. Till it filled the visible glass circular portion, of the pump with a light on top of it, and about 10 ft. tall. To I think maybe about 10 gallons. Then when full, by gravity, gasoline would flow down by hose, when the hose was inserted into the vehicle, and the handle pressed. To the amount of gasoline desired. Oil was also sold, usually pumped from a 50 gallon barrel or sold from bottles with long tapered spouts. By the quart to pour into the engine. Usually most station operators filled autos with gasoline, checked the oil, and cleaned windshields in those days.

Comstocks store also sported a type of electric lights that ran from a charger. With a gasoline engine type charger that charged batteries that would light electric bulb's till the bat- teries got low. Then the batteries had to be charged by the engine ran generator, to charge the batteries again. Some places had that type of light.

That was the two stores in Peacock. Over the years they no longer exist. But memories remain. They served their purpose on life's large stage, quite well when they were there.

MY SPECIAL PLACE

When I was young a special place that I liked to be was to walk on the railroad track. That was easy to do because we lived in a very small town and after the train had went by. It was several hours before another would arrive, and we knew their schedules. So walking on the tracks was safe and easy to do, and also there was miles and miles of railroad track and open space. To walk letting ones imagination wildly soar as desired.

On occasion I could see a deer with its young, sometimes close and sometimes distant. In the trees near the tracks, also many wild berries in the summer. Blue berries, strawberries, june berries, and blackberries that grew nicely along the tracks. Because the old steam engine would blow off steam as it went along on the tracks, which was like rain to the plants and they grew quite well there. The rail-beds were cleaned which helped plants to grow, and my brother, friends, and I would walk for hours. Sometimes eating, gathering berries, eating them and pretending. Just pretending, talking, pretending, about most any treasured childhood thing.

In my special place I could feel the warmth of the Sun's rays in the summer, the coolness of the autumn. The cold snow in winter as the seasons penetrated ones skin. Also raindrops as they fell light sometimes heavy from the sky. Lightning and thunder in the summer could be felt sometimes scary, but nice in a way. Because when it was finished the sun would come out we could usually see rainbows, and rainbows. Are always beautiful and nice, you can almost feel them. They seem close by, but really aren't.

Sometimes I could hear a whippoorwill's call, in near the evening hours. It's permeating lovely, it makes you stop and listen, especially when you're alone. Because it's lonesome, lovely, beautiful, and kind of spiritual in a way and it seems. That even leaves on the tree listen with you. And then there's the night hawk that could be heard in my special place. With its swooping diving call and the rustle of trees. Also a cow bell because some people had cows that roamed freely, throughout the country area.

Our Wedding
Yokohama, Japan
November 30, 1951
Haruko's Mothers House

The smell there was fresh and clean, the smell of country air with nothing but trees and fresh air from nearby hills, with wildflowers. A passing train with its coal smoke, and a few flying cinders mix, with the fresh country air. Of course smoke, coming from chimneys of houses and home cooking, could be smelled at times too.

Sometimes in my special place I would take a cornbread and salt bacon, and butter sandwich. Along with peanut butter and jelly, and disappear where the strawberries, plums, wild plums, blueberries too in the summer, plants in winter were. I remember opening my mouth and tasting snowflakes when they are falling. They are delicious mixed with the country taste of fresh air.

The light there was always bright from the sun, from childhood, from kerosene lamps. There was no electric power in the little town but everything was warmly lit. Lovely I think because I don't remember dark nights. I can feel the mosquito bites, the cold from snow in the winter and damp falling rain. But the feeling is nice, like the touch of warm sunshine on my head. That seems to warm all over, like warm water in a bath tub. It feels good.

In my special place I would run thru the grass chasing butterflies, pretending I was a cowboy. Sometimes a sailor on a pirate ship and it was fun, great fun. But I always wanted to drive a train. I can remember one time one of the engineers let my brother and I climb up in the engine of one of the steam locomotives used back then. He showed us the many gauges where the whistle was, how to ring the bell and a lot of things. I'll always remember that, it was great.

I always wanted to drive a ship to, a submarine, and a motorcycle with a sidecar, and did in my imagination from my special place. An overwhelming feeling I had from my special place was to travel to places far, far away. I used to travel on an imaginary flying carpet in my walks, sometimes from my special place. To places like

China where I would dine with people there, to Egypt and ride camels. To Spain and listened to guitars and then returned to my special place feeling really good. From history books I could read of these places, in my imagination I could travel there, for no one could stop me in my special place.

The old steam trains don't run there anymore but the railroad bed is still there. In Michigan I plan to visit there this summer and see if my magic blanket and imagination can still operate. Because it's really lovely to have a special private place to see, hear, feel, smell, touch. Move and think things in your own private special place. Where you can be, that special you.

Bye

MY WIFE'S A WAR BRIDE (MEANINGFUL LYRICS OF SONGS, MARRIAGE, AND I)

I met my wife in Yokahama Japan in 1948. I was a soldier stationed there. We were married in November 1951 in Yokohama, Japan and remain married, soon will be 58 years. She has been a wonderful wife. We have 3 children, 2 boys and a girl, 7 grandchildren (lost 2 though) and 3 great grandchildren.

The lyrics of the songs popular that I remember from those long ago but not forgotten days are from a Sentimental Journey and Unforgettable.

The Sentimental Journey lyrics I can remember and what they meant to me are:

(lyric)   Gonna take a sentimental journey.

Always meant that I wanted to take a journey back to Japan to be with the lady I wanted to share my life with. Because I had rotated back to America and found my life's love was in Japan. I had to go thru the Korean War to get all the paper work thru for our marriage which was difficult but not im- possible.

(lyric)   Sentimental journey home

Meant to me going back home to my wife someday to be, which later became a reality in Japan

(lyric)   Gonna take a sentimental journey to renew old memories

Meant to me to I was meant to make this journey, marry the lady I desired, to do this would renew our old memories and make many new ones which it has

(lyric)   Gonna take a sentimental journey - sentimental journey home

Meant to me that someday when all the paper work was in order I could take the journey to Japan pick up my wife and we could journey and create our home

The lyrics of the song Unforgettable that I can remember and their meaning to me at that time were as follows:

(lyric)   Unforgettable, that's what you are

The words meant to me that that particular lady I wanted to be my wife was always on my mind and I wanted to be near her care for her and share my life with her

(lyric)   And forever more that's what you'll be

These words meant to me that whatever came or happened she would always have a spot a lovely spot deep very deep in my heart because I wanted and still do to share my life with her

(lyric)   Like a star of love that clings to me

Those words meant like a star in the heavens on a beautiful night seems like a heavenly body if you gaze at it and let its beauty penetrate your senses it will cling fulfill your desire for beauty- for love that is the way my love for this lady was, and still is. *(lyric)*

That my darling's what you mean to me, unforgettable- incredible- to me

These words had the meaning to me that my love and desire for my future wife was as deep as the incredible unforgettable depths of the ocean, or the heights of the heavens, and that it was my desire for this love and desire to remain thru whatever situation or encounter our marriage might have to face.

The wife I met soon 58 years ago has made the Sentimental Journey through, many beautiful Unforgettable years

My graduation classbook class of 1947 Dickson High School Brethren Michigan

EVENTS

There wasn't much exciting going on where I lived, that day. Of course there never was. It's kind of nice at times that way, kind of makes for a peaceful quiet day. I think we had went to the post office and picked up the mail. My father always liked it then because the newspa- per always came in the mail, The Ludington Daily News. It was printed in a little town called Ludington about 35 or 40 miles away which was near Lake Michigan.

We went to that little town I think when I graduated from Dickson High School in Brethren Michigan for our senior trip where we caught a car ferry boat that traveled from Ludington Michigan and across Lake Michigan to Chicago Illinois. We made that trip for our senior graduation to visit the Wrigley Bldg. in Chicago. It was a nice trip. I still remember it. The first time I had ever seen a city that big having spent my growing years in a little town of about 40 people maximum population. I remember my large senior class had 13 graduates total our school vice principal and his wife was in charge of the big class they had no trouble. Except on the return trip a couple of the girls got caught fraternizing with a couple of merchant sea-men in a lifeboat so they didn't get to graduate with us, that was kind of sad, our class was so small.

Another thing I remember from that trip was, for some reason I think our vice principal guide let us have a little time on our own so we boys decided to catch a taxi to go somewhere in Chicago. A lady was driving the taxi. I guess she knew young boys liked to drive recklessly so she decided to shake us up Chicago style. In spots where she could safely do it, she spun the wheels went around corners it felt like on 2 wheels. Sometimes slammed on the brakes, and took us for a grand old teenage ride. Then asked how ya doing boys. We got out and said whew-yow. Thanks. Can't remember if she charged us or not. She first asked us where we were from, and found out we were on our graduation trip from a little Michigan town. Guess she decided to have some fun. It was good, must have been, I still remember the taxi ride. Have ridden in several taxi's in Okiwawa used, painted and resold them with my sons and I used to make extra money in our spare time that way. It also gave us valuable father son time together. But I still for some reason remember that taxi ride. I guess it was because it was dur-ing my senior graduation trip and of all graduations (school graduations) the high school senior graduation seems to be the most important. I guess because you're achieving something you've grown with for 12 years and worked quite hard for. Suddenly it yours.

Back to the first part of this writing when I first started writing about the Ludington Newspaper. Something else happened even before I got carried away writing about the high school graduation trip. I believe I was only about maybe 7 or 8 years, if that old. At that time not too many airplanes flew over in fact one never seen many. Also some were of the bi-plane two wings, one wing over the other type. When an airplane was spotted folks would say there goes an airplane. I remember my father used to say "Look lads, there goes a flying machine". Not like now, they are everywhere. Sometime though you would see a dirigible go by, they made a noise different from an airplane and they seemed to kind of float in the air which to me was very fascinating.

One day I was outside, I can still remember, I heard this engine sound and looking up- here was this huge dirigible with people in the little car under it. They were riding in, pressed against the windows, just looking down seemingly having a grand old time. The dirigible just floated slowly by really low then it went higher and was on its way. I guess, just showing folks, a wee' little town, of poor folks. It made a lasting impression on me, I enjoyed the expe-rience and have since always wanted to ride in a dirigible. After that the Hindenburg dirigible burned I believe in New York and they went obsolete except for a very few the military used some for, or as blimps. Now some few for advertising are used, but not too many. After that thru the growing years, other events, memorable events that occurred: President Kennedys death, Rev. Martin Luther King's death. The now economy trouble it seems the world is hav-ing. That all hopes to soon get better because jobs, work, money is scarce. Crime seems to be on the increase. These things seem to cycle with history.

Events makeup our lives. Must close for now. I've written the sunlight out, it's getting dark and I'm writing above and below the lines and words still seem to be in the pen

But bye for now and till next time.

Hi again,

It's another day, thought of some more events and here they are. Some other events just arrived by thought express quick way to communicate. Very quiet too.

Think I spoke or wrote about my mother raising chickens. One time when she had baby chicks an owl started hanging around, he or she must have spotted the baby chicks or maybe just chickens period anyway we had an owl.

So mother told father about it, we kids listened and watched what would be the action plan father would follow. He always had a plan, seemed for everything. From what I can re-member, he didn't say anything, he just listened, said ok, watched the area, and cut a pole, took his little pull cart 2 wheel wagon went to the close by neighboring forest and cut a tree maybe 10 or 15 ft. in length buried it in a hole about 2 foot deep. I think he waited a few days till the owl got accustomed to using it as a watching place because it was near the chicken house where he watched with a better view, andit was used by the owl. Then my father took the pole down and placed a trap on top, put the pole back up and waited, the next day I think or very soon after, there was the owl in the trap attached to the pole with a chain. Father lowered the pole with attached owl in trap disposed of the owl put the trap away, and went back to his other many daily functions. Think the pole was used as fire wood.

Another event that comes to mind is the wakes that were held when a person died they were usually held in the house where the person lived or a church or another place of choice. Food seemed to be a big part of wakes that I remember. Lots of food could be found there. Every family brought something. People would eat, visit, remember the deceased, events, good and bad, a minister would perhaps say something too. A general good time would be had. The deceased was always in a casket in the house or wherever the wake was held.

The coroner had to pronounce a person dead if they made a mistake and the person was in a deep coma they might awaken in the early days, in the county too. The body was not kept long. Usually not much over 3 days in hot months because of decomposition. Some folks chose not to embalm the corpse when that was possible. So if a person was in a deep coma and the coroner didn't catch everything they might awaken, if it happened during the wake it could shake up the wake.

I remember of talking to a gentleman that told me twice the coroner had pronounced him dead and his body was waiting to be prepared I guess for embalming or whatever. Anyway he awakened, he said it quite shook up the nurses there too. When speaking of it he was working in his garden, and gave me a couple of zucchini squash that day, appeared to be in pretty good health.

In the country there would always be snakes near in the summer months, if one was seen near the house. We knew to leave it alone, go get the snake killer which was something our father made with a handle about 8 or 10 feet long shaped like a large kitchen spatula for turn-ing hot items, only it was sharp on the striking side and one would stand off and cut the snake in half separate the two pieces and dig a hole and bury them.

Most snakes seen were non-poisonous most were yellow and black color called blow snakes or puff adders. They would kind of flatten their head to look like a cobra snake and hiss if they seen you and usually try to get away. But if the snake killer was near, chop, and one less snake,

One time I was working on an old car of mine in a garage I had built. I had dug a pit in the garage where I could get under cars and work on them. This time I was under the auto working, I heard this hiss noise, it sounded like a tire leaking. I looked at the auto wheels, the tires all seemed ok so I kind of ignored the noise. Then I turned my head and there was this blow snake about 3 feet or so long near my arm just looking at me hissing. I promptly got out from under the auto. When I returned with the killer I think he had left, can't remember for sure. But that snake got my attention. I was maybe 15 or 16 years old then. Still a teenager, working on an old 1937 Willys auto of mine. A good teenager car of that era.

Our Wedding
Yokohama, Japan
November 30, 1951
Haruko's Mothers House

Haruko's wedding picture

Haruko and I
On our
wedding day.

Haruko's family,
the minister, and in-laws.

I took leave from the Korean War
a few days to get married.

Haruko and Nicky
Our place in Yokohama, Japan
Maybe late 1951 or 1952

81

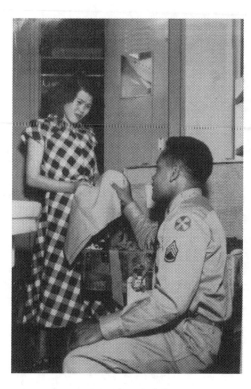

Haruko and I
On board a ship enroute to America from Japan
In 1952, ship maybe named Patrick

My wife Haruko Vicent, My mother Edna May Vicent, Our dog Skippy
Mothers House in 1952
Baldwin, Michigan

Sons - Albert Charles Vicent and William Henry Vicent
Yama-nakako, Japan Maybe 1961-1962 Family vacation in Japan from Okiwawa

Haruko and her mother, Shizuko
Near a banana tree in Okinawa
1963

Buddha Kamakura, Japan Di-a-but-su
Haruko and I, her mother Shizuko,
Brother Hei Jiro and his wife,
and Henry.
Charles maybe took the picture.
Aug 1963

Our friends for years Mr & Mrs. Tucker and Family
Met them in 1956, I believe.

Mosinee Wisconsin
Our friends
Mr. & Mrs. Hoffmann when we visited them at their home in Wisconsin,
maybe 2005, we were friends in the army in Okiwawa for many years

December 31, 1963
VFW Club
Machinato, Okinawa
AirForce S/Sgt. Holland & his wife, Mrs Sadako Holand are with us

When I was Cubmaster of Pack 101 while in the army in Okiwana in 1964 (I think).

Dressed in the Indian uniform as Akela.
I was to be cubmaster for about 2 weeks(I was told)
and had to stay on for about 3 1/2 years,
but both sons Charles and Henry became Cubscouts.
It was a big pack, about 100 boys.
Consisted of 12 Dens
Sponsored by the Am. Legion a very good sponsor in Okiwawa
We had good times.

Haruko dressed in her Kimono
Okinawa, maybe 1963-64

Haruko, our Govt. quarters
Okinawa maybe 1963-64

Haruko and I on the way to a club, evening out or something.
Okinawa 1964-1965

A store in Yama na shi-kin
Shi-zu-mi, Japan

Where Haruko went she was a little girl. The same lady store owner
was there when Haruko, I and the children visited in 1964

Haruko and her mother in Okinawa

Haruko and her mother Vacationing in either Washington or California

Haruko her mother and I Vacationing in either Washington or California

Haruko and I in front of our home 657
Argentine Drive
Salinas, California
Maybe 1974-75
It was near a broccoli field.

Our two son's
Albert Charles Vicent
And
William Henry Vicent
Christmas 1979
Our home 657 Argentine, CA.

Charles is about 25 yrs.
Henry is about 23 yrs.

Charles is leaning on Henries Pachinko game.
Henry liked to play the Japanese
Game Pachinko.

Haruko and I on the beach 1987

New year 2001 picture
Made by Henry

People with eye glasses eyes shine.
All the family in picture except Mariko, Henrys wife, and his daughter Haruka

Acquired two daughter-in-law's
Same day.
Both son's married together
In small chapel near
Coral De Terra
Salinas, CA

91

Haruko and I with Charles at Fairbanks Alaska govt. housing 1954.

*Haruka and I
at our house,
front door area*

*Riding my old, old bicycle with grandchildren Kanna center bicycle, Haruka in
the basket and their friends at our place 657 Argentine Dr. Salinas, Ca
Maybe 1988-89*

The van was my old pop top camper I used it a lot we used it almost every year
for camping the grandchildren usually always went with us. It was my very favorite
vehicle. I really love camping. It was a 1977 volkswagon camper.

ALBERT E. VICENT AND HARUKO VICENT

*In Celebration
of the
Golden Wedding Anniversary of
Albert and Haruko Vicent.*

*You are cordially invited to attend
a luncheon celebrating the
Golden Wedding Anniversary of
Mr. & Mrs. Albert and Haruko Vicent,
honoring 50 years of marriage and
dedication to each other.*

*Date: November 4, 2001 (Sunday)
Time: 1:00—3:00 P.M.
Place: Cathay House Restaurant
213 Monterey Street
Salinas, California 93901
(831) 422-6133*

***This is a SURPRISE Party, please
help us keep it that way by not
discussing with Al or Haruko Vicent.*

1918 Declaration St. Salinas CA. 93906

*Picture for 50ᵗʰ wedding anniversary
(Golden Anniversary) news paper announcement*

*The children held a complete surprise party at a
local restaurant with friends and presents and all.
It was great.*

95

ANTHONY AND RUDOLPH'S TRAVELS

The name was Anthony P. Dragonfly and he lived at Shady Lane in a long low house, No. 116 Shady Lane Avenue, right close to a big donut house. He loved to fly early in the morning when the sun was just coming up, quiet, bright, shiny, and warm. He also especially loved to fly when the sky was blue. Anthony's very good friend was Rudolph M. Hummingbird. Rudolph lived not too far away at Crossroads Soft Moss in a small kind of rickety house with two not so tall plum trees. House No. 129 Crossroads Soft Moss Street, to be exact.

Rudolph could fly really fast and almost stop anywhere. Rudolph would like to fly right after the sun was up a little bit and when the flowers were opening. He then would like to stop at lots of opening flowers and drink their sweet nectar juice.

Sometimes he would meet Anthony Dragonfly and they would stop for awhile and talk because Anthony would usually be coming home from his early morning flying trip, after catching a few bugs and just exercising his wings for the day. After a short visit they usually went their different ways because Anthony Dragonfly like to skim water on the pond near his home looking for bugs and Rudolph had to hurry because he liked drinking nectar from flowers as they opened.

During their brief morning visits they became very good friends and on one visit Rudolph told Anthony Dragonfly about September each year when he always flew back to a place where the weather was warmer for the winter, then fly back here for the summer. Rudolph told Anthony it would be nice if he could go too. He might like it in the winter there. Anthony Dragonfly replied, "Yes, thank you Rudolph, but I could never fly that far or as fast as you Rudolph. I only fly close around here."

Rudolph told Anthony "I've thought about that Anthony. I've seen a train going where I fly. It blows out smoke, has a whistle, and a bell. It goes pretty fast too, and stops at little towns. It has a little red car on the back. We might find nice people on the train to let us ride in the little red car, it would be nice not to have to fly. We could pack our suitcases, take some food and when the train stops, sometimes we could fly around. You find some bugs and I find some flowers with nectar, then we can get back on the train and just ride. How does that sound Anthony? I flew real close to one train. A man in the little red car saw me and said, "Oh look, a hummingbird." That man seemed nice.

Anthony said "It sounds real nice. I could not fly very far, but the train ride sounds nice. I like donuts and I could get plenty of donuts. I know some bee's that have a flower nectar shop."

"You do?" said Rudolph. "That is nice. You have a car too don't you Anthony? Why we can pick up everything and get ready. This is nice! Think about it Anthony, we can talk more about it another time. We have lots of time."

Anthony didn't waste any time, he thought about the trip! Days were nice and warm, it was summer, even the evenings were nice. They always were. Now things were a little different, since his friend Rudolph suggested they take the vacation together. Anthony always stayed close to his home before, but now he thought more about the vacation. "I'll talk to my friend Joseph Crow about our vacation plans, he always goes somewhere."

Joseph's house was not far from Anthony's place. Anthony saw Joseph outside in his yard and stopped to say, "Hello Joseph, how are you? I have not seen you for a very long time."

Joseph said "Yes I've been gone for awhile, my friends and I went up north to where the plums are getting ripe, we had a very nice time, lots of others went too. We flew but many went by train."

"Oh, is that right, by train?" said Anthony.

"Yes, by train" Joseph replied. "There's a very nice train right near here that goes most any place." "I did not know that" Anthony replied, because Anthony always flew everywhere being a dragonfly.

"Joseph," Anthony asked, "How was your vacation? Did you have a good time?"

"Yes we did" Joseph replied. "I think everyone should take a vacation, they are nice, you can rest and see a lot of things." Joseph's friend Alfred Starling, a noisy meddlesome bird, was standing near listening, who liked to talk, spoke up and said, "Yes, I went too. We all had a nice time. I didn't fly all the way though. I rode on the train with the others."

"What is the name of this train?" Anthony asked.

"Why it's the Rabbit Choo Choo, goes all over the place here, and far far away. Bill and his cousin Jerry Rabbit drive it most of the time. Old train goes pretty fast, smokes a lot; you can see the smoke a long way off and hear the whistle."

"Thank you," Anthony replied. "Rudolph, Mr. Hummingbird, my very good friend and I are thinking about going on a vacation together. I can't fly far and fast like he does so he said it might be nice to ride a train that he had seen near here. It must have been the Rabbit Choo Choo."

"Yes," Joseph said, "Ride the train, I think you'll like it. That must have been the Rabbit Choo Choo Rudolph saw; I think that's the only train around here close by."

Anthony told everybody "thank you, but I must go now. I have to do some work at home. Good to know vacations are nice."

Alfred Starling said loudly, "You can find the Rabbit Choo Choo station easy, at Shady Lane Avenue go to Sunrise Drive, then turn left on Sunset, fly over the hill, and you will see the station close to the bridge."

"Thank you Alfred" said Anthony.

The next day Anthony went to the train station and found out the Rabbit Choo Choo train was pretty nice. The station master told Anthony the train always had an open flat car that Anthony could put his car on. This way Anthony could use his car on his vacation then bring it back home.

The station master also told Anthony that he and Rudolph could sit in their car and ride if they wanted to. Anthony said, "my car has no top. I am so tall and my car is so small."

"That is okay" said the station master. "You can both use your parasols." Anthony was very happy and told the station master thank you and went home to tell Rudolph the good news about their vacation plans.

Rudolph was not home when Anthony got there. That was okay because, some of Anthony's friends came by. They had a good time just flying around catching a few bugs and having dragonfly races. Dragonflies can fly pretty fast Anthony thought. 'I'll have to tell my friend Rudolph he can stop over with us and maybe see how fast we fly. It would be fun, lots of fun, I also that way could see friends I had not seen for a long time.

The next day Anthony saw Rudolph and told him about having talked to several friends and how they all had a good time on vacation. Rudolph listened as Anthony talked. When Anthony finished, Rudolph asked Anthony if he wanted to go on vacation with him. Anthony said, "Yes, I'll go. I never went on a vacation before. It sounds like fun, and the train ride with my car should be nice."

Rudolph said, "In about two more weeks I'll be ready to go. That will give us time to get everything we want to take with us ready."

September seemed to come fast this year, maybe because of the vacation they planned to take together. Anthony had his car checked to be sure it was okay and it was in good shape. The auto shop told Anthony to be sure and park the car where it would always get plenty of sunshine, because Anthony's car runs on sunshine.

Rudolph went to Anthony's place and tasted some donuts because Anthony lived by the donut shop. Anthony planned to take donuts to eat on the train, so Rudolph wanted to taste the donuts and sweet nectar from Anthony's friend's shop.

Rudolph liked the donuts, especially the plain donuts, and the chocolate flavored ones. Anthony also liked the sweet nectar from Anthony's friends shop, known as the Bee Shop.

Rudolph told Anthony to be sure and bring donuts and sweet nectar so they could eat them on the train.

Rudolph also told Anthony, "don't worry Anthony; I know plenty of places where we can find water holes with lots of bugs you can catch easy. I've seen them when I fly there all the time."

The two weeks went by real fast and Anthony Dragonfly and Rudolph Hummingbird were ready to leave on vacation. They got the tickets, loaded Anthony's car, and put the sweet nectar and donuts in Anthony's car so they could eat some anytime. The car was easy to put on the Rabbit Choo Choo flat car because Anthony just drove it up a little ramp and right on the train where it was tied down tight with special strong grape vines. The station master said at every station Anthony could drive the car off easily if he wanted.

All of Anthony and Rudolph's friends came to the train station to see their friends leave. They told them to have a nice vacation. Even Ollie Crocodile and Shorty Giraffe came.

Anthony and Rudolph climbed into Anthony's car on the Rabbit Choo Choo train. The train used sun- shine for power, just like Anthony's car. It kept sunshine in a sunshine car to make the train go. Anthony's car kept sunshine in a little small box to make it run.

Anthony and Rudolph waved at their friends and away they went as the Rabbit Choo Choo train chugged off. The train rolled along, moving through the country past little houses, streams, just beautiful places.

Anthony said, "You know Rudolph, this is really nice. We just sit and it's kind of like a movie, you just watch everything. I like it. Look at those flowers, and the green grass, and the hills, and the trees. When we fly we see it too, we fly so fast we don't really think about it, but the train goes slow and we can really look at it and enjoy it more."

Rudolph answered, "Yes, I really like it; it's slow, and you can see everything. When I fly, I fly fast and stop to drink nectar from plants like those over there. Look Anthony, at that little pond over there. There must be lots of tasty bugs you could catch there. This vacation idea is really nice. I like it."

"Looking at those flowers makes me hungry" said Rudolph. "How about the nectar you brought and the donuts? Let's eat. How about you Anthony, aren't you a little hungry?"

"Yes" said Rudolph. "Let's eat. Here's the nectar Rudolph and I'll eat some donuts."

"You might like them too" said Anthony. "I just love donuts. Try some Rudolph."

"I think I will Anthony, donuts are pretty good. Next time I have flower nectar I'll come back and have a donut."

"That's good Rudolph" said Anthony, "There's plenty of donuts right here in this bag, help yourself anytime. The trains slowing down, maybe we're going to stop. "

"Oh yes, we are Rudolph" said Anthony. "This might be good because we just passed that pond where you said there might be a lot of bugs for me and plants with nectar for you. We can take off the car and drive back there. That would be real nice."

"Hey, we're going to stop and here comes Jerry Rabbit. Hi Jerry Rabbit."

"I Wonder why he's walking fast, hope everything's ok. It looks like he wants to talk with us."

"Hi Jerry" said Rudolph. "Is this a regular stop?"

"Oh yes, it is" said Jerry "I came to tell you because I remember when your car was put on the train; you said you would like to get off at long stops and take your car and look around. This is about a 2 hour stop. So take your car and have a good time. I have to get back to the engine with Bill. We're going to a little restaurant we know and it serves good fresh carrot and celery salad, makes you hungry driving this train all day.

"Thanks for letting us know Jerry,"said Rudolph. "Enjoy your salad at the restaurant."

"You're welcome" said Jerry. "We wanted to make sure you knew we would be here for 2 hours.

Since you are out here with your car with no speaker you couldn't hear the news." Jerry then went back to work.

Anthony and Rudolph got everything ready, had gotten in the car and were about to leave, when Ru- dolph looked up and heard two birds calling their name.

"Anthony, Rudolph, Anthony, Rudolph!"

Rudolph said, "Anthony that looks like our friends Alfred Starling and Oscar Crow! It is our friends. I wonder what they want. Hope its good news."

When Oscar and Alfred landed they said they had chased the train for about 2 days to tell Alfred and Rudolph that Ollie Crocodile wanted them to know that his cousin Andy Alligator runs a ferry boat service at Happy Happy Lake Resort.

"It goes around the resort on the lake over to Flower Bug Island," Ollie said, "It's a really nice place and so is the island, so stop there if you can and be sure to tell Andy Alligator hi from Ollie Crocodile, his cousin. We must go now Anthony and Rudolph. Have a nice vacation. Glad we caught up to you vacation travelers."

"Thank you Oscar and Alfred. We'll stop there, please tell Ollie thank you and have a good time flying back home" said Rudolph.

When they left, Anthony told Rudolph that it was nice Oscar and Alfred flew so far to bring them that information and good that Ollie Crocodile remembered they were on vacation. "We will enjoy Happy Happy Resort so we must stop there and see Ollie's cousin, Andy Alligator," said Anthony.

"Of course," said Rudolph "We have to do that."

Then Anthony drove off the train flat car and he and Rudolph were off to look at the little town. As they drove along Anthony saw a sign, "SEE A DEEPY CREEPY CAVE."

Anthony asked Rudolph, "Rudolph did you see that sign?"

"Yes," Rudolph answered "I saw it. Let's stop and take a look."

Anthony stopped the car, both got out and walked to the office. A large beaver named Tom worked there and told them, "Hi I'm Tom Beaver, can I help you?"

Rudolph said, "We would like to visit the Deepy Creepy Cave!"

"Ok," said Tom Beaver, "Its free today. Terry Turtle will take you through." Tom called Terry the Turtle. Terry came over and said "Climb on my back." Tom gave Anthony and Rudolph two lanterns with fireflies inside.

"When it's dark in the cave the fireflies will give light and you can see. Hang on to the lanterns," Said Tom.

"Ok" Anthony and Rudolph said.

Then Terry started walking up a little path through some bushes and into the cave. Terry kept walking.

The path went down, down, down. Deeper, deeper, deeper till they were down very, very, very deep. The fireflies made the lanterns nice and bright so Anthony and Rudolph could see ok.

Then one of the fireflies said, "I'm tired, I'm going to rest" and the lanterns went out. All the fireflies went to sleep, and it got very dark. Terry Turtle hollered at the fireflies, "Hey you guys wake up!," but all the fireflies were asleep.

Terry said, "That's okay, I know the way." Then suddenly, Terry yelled, "Hang on tight guys, its wet here. We're going to slide a long way. They slid for a long, long way, always deeper, deeper, deeper in the cave. They suddenly bumped into something and stopped. Terry started walking again and said, "You guys okay?" Anthony and Rudolph said, "We're okay; how about you Terry?"

Terry replied, "I'm okay, I kind of liked the slide. Did you keep the lanterns?"

Anthony and Rudolph said, "Yes, we did"

Terry said, "That's good; those fireflies will probably wake up soon and give us some light. Oh yes, pretty soon you may hear some strange noises. I know it's very dark with no lanterns, but don't be too afraid. No one has ever been hurt yet, but we don't know what or who makes the noise when we walk by."

For a very long time, Anthony and Rudolph heard a noise like someone was walking close behind Terry. Then, all of a sudden, Anthony and Rudolph heard the noise turn and go the other way. It was very scary.

Then they heard a scraping noise like someone was scraping a cake pan. It kept going on for a long time. Then, a dragging sound, like someone was dragging a big bag or something for a long time.

Then all of the noise stopped!

All the time, Terry kept walking deeper, deeper, deeper into the cave. It was very dark too, because all the fireflies were resting, and there was no light.

Terry asked, "You guys okay? Did you hear all the noises?"

Anthony and Rudolph said, "Yes we did, and it was very scary."

"I know; we don't know who makes the noises. They seem to like to do that, but they never hurt anybody. Hang on, you'll like the next part," said Terry.

About the time Terry the Turtle finished talking, a large pair of hands picked up Terry, Anthony, and Rudolph. You could hear feet running, but could not hear anyone breathing, just the hands holding Terry the Turtle, Anthony, and Rudolph. They also felt wind and soft noise like wings flapping. It felt good. And very soon they were back almost at the entrance of the cave where Terry had started their adventure. It was still too dark to see.

Then the hands set everybody down and you could hear the sound of footsteps walking away. The fireflies soon awakened and said "We're all rested now" and gave a good light.

Terry listened and told the fireflies, "Next time, don't do that. We needed light in the cave."

The fireflies said, "Sorry, but we were tired."

Terry asked Anthony and Rudolph, "How did you like Deepy Creepy Cave?" Anthony and Rudolph both said that it was good, but scary too.

Terry kept walking. Soon they were out in the sunlight and saw Tom Beaver who also asked them how they liked Deepy Creepy Cave, both told Tom it was good fun. They needed to get back to the train so they told everybody thank you, got in Anthony's car, said goodbye, and left.

Rudolph said, "Anthony, we'd better go back to the train. It's getting late, and we only could stay for two hours. We'd better hurry." Anthony drove pretty fast, and when they got there, the train was waiting. Anthony drove onto the flat car, tied his car down with the grape vine, and soon the Rabbit Choo Choo was moving again.

It was a nice day; the train moved along very nicely. Rudolph and Anthony were tired from their visit in the cave, so they rested and slept for a little while, in fact almost two hours. When Rudolph awakened, he noticed the train was going up a pretty big hill. Rudolph wanted Anthony to see the hills too because there were no big hills where Anthony lived. So Rudolph awakened Anthony, all the time saying, "Look, look Anthony! We are in the hill area, big big hills."

"Anthony I usually fly over these hills when I go to my place in the winter and I never really pay much attention to these hills. But to see them from a train, they are beautiful. What do you think of the hill's Anthony?"

Anthony kept looking. He never saw anything like this before and he told Rudolph, "I have never seen big hills before. This is just beautiful. I'll have to tell Alfred Starling and Oscar Crow about this so they can come see this sometime too."

The Rabbit Choo Choo kept going up, up, up in the hills. Anthony and Rudolph just looked. Anthony did not know what to say, so he said nothing, he just looked and looked at the hills. Then he saw something really different. The ground all covered with white and he said, "Rudolph! Rudolph! What is that white stuff all over the ground on the hills over there?"

Rudolph said, "Oh that? That is snow."

Anthony said, "I have never seen snow, I hope the train stops somewhere near here for a little while so we can go over and look at snow. It is pretty to see. I have never seen anything like that before. "

"I fly this way sometime" said Rudolph. "On the other side of this mountain there is no snow, it's only on the top. I can't fly that high. I don't fly that high but I see the snow when I pass here. Pretty soon we will be where I stay for the winter."

While Rudolph was talking Bill, one of the engineers, came and told Anthony, "Hi, Jerry, and I drive the train. I was just checking the train, just passing through, not much to talk about. Keep doing everything the same."

"Nice trip so far, everything ok here," said Anthony.

"Yes" Bill told them. "We'll be stopping soon at Chilly Station. Be there for 3 hours. Engine needs more sunshine. It was hard pulling coming up the hillside. You might want to take your car and drive around a little when we stop at Chilly Station. If you go to the mountain be careful in the snow. It's different to drive in and it will be cold there too. Do you have jackets?"

Anthony and Rudolph asked each other about jackets and remembered they had put jackets in their bags. So they told Bill the train driver, "Thank you for reminding them about the jackets, they will remember to take jackets with them when they leave to go see the snow."

Bill replied, "You are very welcome, I must go now. We are getting near Chilly Station and Jerry needs me to help, especially since we are in the mountains. I just put speakers in your car. Now you can hear all the announcements too."

"Thank you" said Anthony.

Soon Anthony and Rudolph could feel the train slowing down and heard over the speakers, "Next stop Chilly Station. We will be there for 3 hours. We will be there for 3 hours. We will be there for 3 hours! The engine needs more sunshine. We are using more sunshine pulling in the mountains, our fuel is low. Next stop Chilly Station!"

When the train stopped at Chilly Station, Anthony and Rudolph quickly took off the strong grapevine tied to Anthony's car, got in and drove off the train's flatcar on to the platform which leads down to the street. They were now off to see snow.

Anthony and Rudolph had never seen snow before. "Rudolph," Anthony said "we must stop and put on our jackets; I'm getting cold."

"Yes, and so am I" said Rudolph. "Let's put on our jackets." After they put on their jackets, Rudolph said "These jackets feel good; let's go see the snow Anthony."

Anthony drove on and they saw some deer by the roadside. The mother deer had some babies and they noticed the father deer looked up as they approached.

Anthony stopped and said, "Hello everyone. We are off to see the snow."

Father deer said "That is nice. The snow is beautiful, but be careful; the snow is slippery." "We will," said Anthony.

Anthony told the deer family thank you and goodbye and drove on. Soon they passed a family of friends eating. Some partridges, doves, and blue jays were talking and having a good time.

Anthony stopped and told them, "We are going to see the snow."

The doves told Anthony and Rudolph, "That is nice; have a good time with the good weather. This is the Hoppity Mountain Range. The snow is mostly on the Great Hoppity mountains, so be careful!" The par- tridges and blue jays also said to be careful.

Anthony and Rudolph thanked everybody, waved, and drove on. Soon they came to the snow. An- thony told Rudolph, "It's beautiful over here; we are almost to the top. The road is pretty good." Soon they saw a mountain goat but Anthony didn't stop. As he approached, he blew the horn and waved as he slowed the car down to say, "Hello, we are looking at the snow."

The mountain goat said, "Have a good time," as Anthony drove on.

Then Rudolph said, "Look at the beautiful trees and everything we can see far from here. Oh look Anthony, that sign says top of Hoppity Mountain. Let's turn back." Anthony started to turn around in a bad place, because under the snow was some ice which caused the car to slide into some bushes and get stuck in the snow. The wheels just spun in the snow.

Anthony said, "Rudolph, we are stuck. What will we do? We only had three hours before the train was leaving ... we only have about an hour left."

About that time, a friendly squirrel in a nearby tree eating acorns he saved from the summer was watching from his tree house. He hollered down, "Hello, I'm Jimminy Squirrel; could I come help in any way?"

"Yes you could, I'm Anthony P. Dragonfly and my friend here is Rudolph M. Hummingbird, were just passing by on the Rabbit Choo Choo Train with our car. The train stopped, and we are driving around looking at the beautiful Hoppity Mountains, and now we're stuck in the snow. We would be very happy if you could give us a push."

Jimminy Squirrel said, "I would be happy to do that, and I'll bring my friend Quickly Rat with me, since he's visiting with me today. We'll be right down. Come on Quickly, let's go!"

"Okay," said Quickly, he had been listening and watching too. Soon they were down and pushed An- thony's car out of the snow. Anthony gave them each a donut with a little flower nectar that Anthony had in the car. They said thank you, waved goodbye, and Anthony and Rudolph were on their way back down Hop- pity Mountain.

The car went down the mountain quite fast and they passed everybody that they had seen coming up the mountain. They blew their horn and waved as they said goodbye. Soon they were back to Chilly Station and drove their car up the ramp back onto the flatcar, tied it down with the strong grapevine, and the Rabbit Choo Choo was moving again.

Anthony and Rudolph said, "that was nice; I enjoyed seeing Hoppity Mountain and the Hoppity Mountain Range. They were beautiful, and everyone we met there was nice. I think the next stop will be Happy Happy Lake Resort where Andy Alligator, Ollie Crocodile's cousin, works. I think the train stays there for about three days. If it does, that will be good because we can have Andy Alligator take us to the Flower Bug Island that we have heard so much about since he runs a ferry service there."

"Yes, that will be great" said Rudolph. "I'm glad you remembered. We *must* see that island."

"Anthony," Rudolph said, "It won't be long after we leave Happy Happy Lake Resort before we get to the place where I stay all winter."

"That will be so nice Rudolph, I can hardly wait. This has been a very nice trip so far and I have really enjoyed the train ride. This is the first time I ever rode on a train and the Rabbit Choo Choo, is so nice. The dining car is so nice too."

"Yes," said Rudolph, "The carrot celery soup we had today was delicious."

"It really was," said Anthony. "Those Red Squirrels that do most of the cooking are good cooks."

"Anthony, isn't the train going very slowly? Say, we just stopped. Why, I wonder why! There is no station here. *Why did we stop?*"

"I don't know Rudolph" Anthony answered.

About that time, an announcement came over the train speaker system. "The train has been held up by the Rabbit Cowboys. They are fox-riding cowboys; you may see some of the cowboys near your car wandering around. I will put the leader on the speaker system, he wants to say something."

"Hello everybody, my name is Hector and I'm the leader of the Rabbit Cowboys. We held up your train because we want your carrot celery soup! We have brought our soup tank wagon, so this won't take long and we'll be gone if your cooks cooperate and give us the soup with no trouble."

"We know you have the soup because our look-out Rabbits have been sniffing and know you're cooking carrot celery soup on this train and we want some, but not all. We will leave you enough to get to Happy Happy Lake Resort, but no more."

Anthony said, "Oh, look over there Rudolph at the foxes pulling that wagon with the rabbit driving. That must be the tank wagon the leader talked about."

"Yes Anthony, I think it is" said Rudolph.

Then, Hector came back on the speaker system and said, "Thank you for the soup. Goodbye." And the Rabbit Choo Choo started moving again.

Anthony said, "Rudolph I think that's terrible. Those cowboy bandits should be stopped. I'll tell my friend Ernie Eagle about this, he goes fishing at the little lake near here all the time. The nerve of those Cowboy Rabbits to hold up this train."

"You know Rudolph, I just got a good idea. Your friend Ernie Eagle flies really high and really quiet and he can see a long way. Maybe he could watch the Rabbit Choo Choo sometimes and when these Rabbit Cowboys come by to rob the train, he could swoop down, pick up a cowboy, and drop the cowboy in the water at the Happy Happy Lake Resort; which is close to here."

"Yes Anthony, that's a good idea. It would serve those Rabbit Cowboys right" said Rudolph.

"The next time I see Ernie Eagle I'll ask him if he will do that. He will probably laugh and say, "Of course I will, that will be fun to do. Ernie's a good friend and he will be glad to help" said Rudolph.

"Oh yes Anthony, did you notice each Rabbit Cowboy had a bow and arrow on his shoulder?"

"No, I didn't notice that Rudolph." "I did" said Rudolph.

"Those Rabbit Cowboys really wanted that soup. Maybe they are sitting around a big campfire, eating their stolen carrot celery soup right now" said Anthony.

And that is just what they were doing, keeping all the other animals close by grumbling, awake, and angry. But the Rabbit Cowboys didn't care. They told the other animals 'Oh be quiet, we don't care; we are having fun."

The train moved along slowly, but nice and smooth. Anthony and Rudolph just looked at the country pass by as the train moved.

Then Rudolph said, "Anthony, I fly this way sometimes but there is not too much out here other than some rabbits, squirrels and birds."

Anthony replied, "Yes, it looks pretty quiet out here."

About that time, the train started to slow some more and the conductor came over the speaker saying,

"Next stop will be Happy Happy Lake Resort. We will be here for three days."

When the train stopped Anthony told Rudolph, "Let's go to the room that I made a reservation for. We can rest tonight and find Andy Alligator, Ollie Crocodile's cousin, tomorrow. Then we can catch his ferry to Flower Bug Island and stay there for two days before returning to the train and then it's off to your winter rest place at Nicely Nice Winter Rest."

After a very good night's rest, Anthony woke up first then woke up Rudolph.

"Rudolph, let's go eat. I'm hungry. I saw a nice breakfast pond on one side and flowers with nectar on the other side. I'll eat on the pond side and you can find nectar on the other side. Let's meet here when we finish and go find Andy Alligator, Ollie's cousin, and catch the ferry to Flower Bug Island."

"Sounds like a good idea" said Rudolph. "Let's go eat breakfast; I'm hungry too."

Rudolph finished eating first and waited just a little while for Anthony to return. "Anthony," Rudolph said, "How was breakfast?"

Anthony said, "Very good, the pond had lots of bugs. How was your breakfast?"

"Good, good, I mean very good too. The flowers had lots of nectar. This place has lots of good things to eat. Now let's go find Andy Alligator and his ferry service to Flower Bug Island."

As they headed for the ferry boat, they saw a kangaroo hopping along, so they flew low and asked the kangaroo about Andy Alligator's ferry boat service.

"Oh yes," the kangaroo replied, "I'm Kindy Kangaroo, and I work there. It's about six good hops away¼follow me!"

They were soon at the ferry boat office where Andy was sitting outside in the sunshine waiting for customers. Rudolph and Anthony went right over, met Andy Alligator, and told him they were Ollie Crocodile's friends. They said Ollie had told them to look Andy his cousin the ferry boat operator up and tell him hello and be sure to visit Flower Bug Island.

Andy said, "Thank you, and when you go back tell Ollie hello from me, Andy Alligator." "We'll do that," said Rudolph and Anthony.

"Now," Andy said, "Let me take you to Bug Island. Are you ready?" "Yes, let's go" Rudolph and Anthony replied.

"Follow me" said Andy. "See that big log in the water? Hop on and I'll push you to Flower Bug Island. That log is the ferry." With Andy pushing, soon they were at Flower Bug Island.

"Here we are" said Andy. "There is a lot to see here and plenty to eat. There are lots of bugs, flowers with delicious nectar, beautiful sunrises and sunsets to see, fish swimming by, even an old shipwreck on the other side of the island that's been there for years.

"There is also a little train that runs around the island. It's free, everything at Happy Happy Resort is free, like the Rabbit Choo Choo. Everything is free; it all comes from sunshine kept in big sunshine tanks.

"Enjoy everything, be careful, and have fun."

"See you in two days. Thank you and bye" Anthony and Rudolph told Andy. Anthony left his car on the train because it would be too much trouble to take to Flower Bug Island on the ferry, so they walked a little and looked at the island. Then the island train came.

"Let's catch the train and look at the island" said Rudolph.

"Yes" said Anthony, "That's the best way to see it."

"This is a pretty big island" said Anthony. "What is that big building over there? It looks empty."

The train driver heard Anthony and said, "This island, a very long time ago, was kept by a lot of pirates. They made the buildings."

A red squirrel was driving the little train and said, "People never come here." The driver kept talking and said, "Sometimes when you look at the old buildings you can see people, but when you go over there, nobody is there. Over there, see the seals playing and laying in the sun? There are lots of fish on this side jumping, playing, and eating. Sometimes our friend Ernie the Eagle comes here and fishes. He's very nice. Everybody likes Ernie."

Rudolph said, "Ernie, he's my friend too, I've known Ernie a long time. Anthony and I were just talking about him yesterday when the Rabbit Cowboys held up the train for carrot celery soup. We were saying it would be nice if Ernie could catch one of those bandit cowboys and drop him in the lake. Wouldn't that be nice?"

"Oh yes" the driver said "There is always talk about those Rabbit Cowboys. They are quite a bunch of bad guys."

Rudolph said, "I hope we get to see Ernie while we're here or at Nicely Nice Winter Rest. That's where were going. That's the next stop I think."

"Yes it is" said the driver. "I'm sure you'll see Ernie. He comes around here all the time. Since this is your first visit to Flower Bug Island and it's early in the morning, I'm in no big hurry."

The driver said "I'll just point out some of the things to see. You can come back and look at them if you stay for 1 or two days."

"We'll be here for two days," said Anthony.

As the train moved along, on the left side was Lookout Mountain, from there you can see over most of the island. "You can see where the seals and fish play. All over the island, there are lot s of bugs and many beautiful flowers. As we move along you can see that old building. It's called the Old Castle. It's empty, but since you guys can fly you can fly over and look in it. That should be fun. Oh by the way everyone just calls me Red. I'm from the Red Squirrel Family," the driver said.

"Thank you" said Rudolph, "My name is Rudolph and my friends name is Anthony. Thank you Red for showing us so many interesting things to see."

"I have told you about most of the things to seen on Flower Bug Island but you have to see the Twilight Rainbow before you leave. You must be close to the Old Castle building to see it and if you look down near the beach when the Twilight Rainbow comes, the mermaids will come out to watch the rainbow. That is the only time you ever see the mermaids when the rainbow finishes they stay a little while and then go back into the water."

"We must see the Twilight Rainbow before we leave," said Anthony.

"There's a little place near the castle you might want to stay the night at since there are lots of flowers and bugs. Anywhere in this place there isn't a bad spot to watch the Twilight Rainbow but two days will go fast. You can take your time, fly around and I will be close by with the train when you are ready to leave."

"Thank you Red, we'll do that," said Anthony.

"Sounds good Rudolph"

"Thanks Red"

Red left with the train. Anthony and Rudolph found the place near the castle that Red spoke of. Rudolph had lots of flower nectar and Anthony had a lot of bugs. They rested and then flew around and came back to the old castle. Both days they watched the Twilight Rainbow and the mermaids. The mermaids watched Anthony and Rudolph as they all watched the Twilight Rainbow together. Then the mermaids would play a little in the water near the beach and go back into the water.

The mermaids had long black hair and faces and arms like people. They lived in the water near the old castle. Anthony and Rudolph had never seen them anywhere else. Rudolph and Anthony spent two days on Flower Bug Island but came back each day to the rest area by the old castle to watch the Twilight Rainbow with the mermaids. They thought they saw people near the castle but never did even though Rudolph could fly and stand still in the air. As he flew, he would stop in mid-air and look into the old castle windows. The beds were all made up nice like someone was there but they never saw anyone. It was the same with the old ship wreck, no one was around.

Anthony and Rudolph flew and rode the train all over the island and had a good time. They thanked the island train driver Red, and said, "We enjoyed the visit especially the Twilight Rainbow and the strange visit with the castle mermaids."

Then they went to the ferry place and Andy Alligator was waiting with his ferry. He asked them if they enjoyed the visit on Flower Bug Island. Anthony and Rudolph told Andy thank you and the visit to Flower Bug Island was very nice.

Soon they were back to Happy Happy Lake Resort and told Andy Alligator thank you and that they would tell Ollie Crocodile hello from Andy Alligator. Then they got back on the Rabbit Choo Choo and continued on their way to Nicely Nicely Winter Rest. The three day stop over at Happy Happy Lake Resort was nice. Everyone had a nice rest and looked forward to the rest of the trip to Nicely Nicely Winter Rest.

After the Rabbit Choo Choo Train traveled around huge Happy Happy Lake and got out of the Hoppity Mountain Range, everything was nice.

Rudolph said, "Anthony this is where a lot of my eagle friends live. I think this is where Ernie is from. I do hope we get to see Ernie while we are here this winter."

Anthony answered "I certainly want to meet Ernie, I'm sure we will."

"Anthony" Rudolph said "I know this place very well, because I come here every winter. We will be there soon. It's not far after we leave Happy Happy Lake Resort. I'm sure you will like Nicely Nicely Winter Rest. Most everyone comes here for winter"

Then the Rabbit Choo Choo started to slow and the conductor said "Next stop Nicely Nicely Winter Rest."

When the train stopped, Anthony and Rudolph removed the very strong grapevine holding Anthony's car down and carefully drove off the ramp. Rudolph showed Anthony where to go for their winter vacation place, Nicely Nicely Winter Rest.

"Drive this way" Rudolph told Anthony. "Turn at the next corner. Keep going straight till I tell you to stop."

"Alright" Anthony said.

They had not gone too far when Rudolph said, "This big lake we are passing is Lake Nicely. Lots of my good friends live here. There's Rupert Bullfrog, Homer Cricket, Tony Turtle, and of course my long time friend Mr. Willie Skunk and Kathy Katydid."

"At the next corner turn left Anthony."

"Ok," said Rudolph turning before he forgot.

"Rudolph you have lots of friends here?"

"Oh yes," said Rudolph "I've been coming here for a long time." "That's nice," said Anthony.

"Thank you Anthony, I'm sure you will meet a lot of new friends here also, seems everyone does. This big place on the right side is a big open hotel where everybody stays. It's all free. All you have to do is use plenty of sunshine every day. If you have cars or anything like that, keep it filled all the time and use plenty of sunshine. If you don't your friends are supposed to check on you and find out why. So remember Anthony, use plenty of sunshine and keep your car filled with sunshine everyday so you and your car are ready to go anytime. Remember everything is free. "

At just about twilight, right before evening every night, "The choir starts singing. Almost everybody and anybody can sing and everyone wants you to sing as long as you want. I know my friends all sing except Willie Skunk. I don't think I have ever heard him sing," said Rudolph.

"We can park your car almost anywhere since there's not many cars here, most just fly in or catch the Rabbit Choo Choo."

"Oh there's a different car. I have never seen that one before. That's Rupert Bullfrog. He sings base in the choir at night. I must tell him hello" said Rudolph "This is the first time I have seen him on this visit."

"Hello Rupert," said Rudolph "Good to see you."

"Good to see you too Rudolph."

"This is my friend Anthony. He came with me for vacation this time. Anthony this is Rupert," said Rudolph. They exchange greetings of nice to meet each other.

"We came on the Rabbit Choo Choo train. It was a nice ride," said Anthony. "Where did you get the car Rupert?" said Rudolph.

"Oh," said Rupert "a friend gave it to me. He drove it down from somewhere, got tired of it and I've been using it. I used to come on the train all the time too but I will probably take my car back this time though. You two could ride back too if you want to send your car back by train. It's all free."

"We'll think about it. Thanks Rupert. Nice to see you again Rupert," said Rudolph.

"Same here," said Rupert, "And nice to meet you Anthony." "Nice to meet you too Rupert," said Anthony.

"Oh say Rupert," said Rudolph "Have you seen Ernie Eagle?"

"Yes I did," said Rupert "I saw him yesterday. He was fishing in the lake near me. He landed and I swam over and we talked for a long time. In fact we talked about you. I wondered when you would get here on vacation."

"That's nice," said Rudolph. "When you see him again tell him hello and that we're here and would like to see him."

"I'll do that," said Rupert. "Bye."

Then Rudolph and Anthony flew down a couple of blocks. Rudolph pointed out a place filled with lots of bugs.

"This is another one of our outdoor restaurants. There are several of these so you can eat anytime you want too."

"Let's just fly around some and look at the place," said Rudolph. "It's a pretty big place and the weather here is nice too. It is a very nice place for the winter. Say, that must be Ernie over there. Let's fly by and tell him hello," said Rudolph, "And I can introduce you to Ernie."

"Let's do that," said Rudolph.

When they got over where Ernie was sitting, Ernie was surprised and said, "Hi Rudolph, Rupert Bull-frog and I were talking about you the other day and wondering when you would get here."

"Well here we are Ernie. This is my friend Anthony Dragonfly. I invited him to come on vacation. Anthony this is Ernie Eagle."

Ernie and Anthony exchanged greetings of "nice to meet you." Then Rudolph told Ernie it took them a little longer because they rode the Rabbit Choo Choo train.

"Oh that's nice," said Ernie. "I see it a lot. Rupert Bullfrog said he rides it too sometimes."

"Yes he told us yesterday when we saw him. He said he rides it sometimes but yesterday he was driving a car. He said his friend had given him the car," said Rudolph.

Ernie said "Oh yes he does drive the car. I can't ride in his car. It's too small for me, I'd rather fly anyway. I like to fly high and see everything."

"Oh Ernie, there was something I wanted to tell you. When we came on the Rabbit Choo Choo near Happy Happy Lake Resort those pesky Rabbit Cowboys held up the train and stole some of the carrot celery soup. I was thinking, it would be nice if sometime you were flying by that way if you could kind of keep watch from above. If you see those cowboys robbing the train riding foxes and using them to pull their wag on that carries the carrot celery soup they steal, we thought maybe you could swoop down, pick up one of the cowboys, fly over Happy Happy Lake Resort and drop him in the lake. Serve him right. He could swim out all wet and walk home. What do you think about that Ernie?"

Ernie said, "Rudolph that sounds like great fun. I'd just love to do that. I catch fish like that all the time. I've never caught a Rabbit Cowboy like that before but it would be easier than catching a fish. And then to carry him high in the air and drop him in the lake wow, that would just be lots of vacation fun. Why don't both of you hop on? Let's go take a little fly around the place. I'm sure we can find out where those cowboys stay. I've heard about them and we can see the entire vacation place too. You guys hang on good though. Kind of stick your feet under my feathers and hang on."

Ernie spread his big wings and away they went. Ernie flew real high then he called back to Anthony and Rudolph, "Everything ok back there?"

"Everything's fine" said Anthony and Rudolph, "We're just enjoying the ride. You could fly a little lower and then we can see better."

"Ok" said Ernie "I'm used to flying high but I'll just spread my wings and not flap them so much and glide around up here. Have a good time. Maybe we can see the Rabbit Choo Choo train and maybe those Rabbit Cowboys will be around too. If they are bothering the train I'll glide down real quiet, pick up the bad guy, drop him in the water over in the Happy Happy Lake and you guys can watch."

"Sounds like fun. I'd really like to do that. Let's go see if we can find the Rabbit Choo Choo and see if everything is ok."

"Yes let's go," said Anthony and Rudolph. "Ok," said Ernie "We'll keep gliding around and I'll keep looking and see if we can find the train and if it's ok."

Ernie circled around gracefully. "Look at the Nicely Nice Winter Rest. It's really a nice place with lots of flowery wet places. There are a lot of nice and quiet looking restful places. It really looks nice. I think you will like it here Anthony. You should have a nice relaxing vacation. We like it here don't we Rudolph?" said Ernie.

"I think it is too. I certainly got a nice look at the whole place looking down while you circled over from high in the sky. It looks nice and thank you Ernie," said Anthony.

Oh look at what I just saw. The Rabbit Choo Choo train and it's stopped way out here. There's no station or anything out there. Let's go down and see if everything is ok," said Ernie.

"I can see what is wrong now" said Ernie "The Rabbit Cowboys have held up the train again. I can see them walking around. They use foxes to ride on."

"Just hang on tight now, Rudolph your idea of picking up a cowboy and dropping him in the water, I think I can do that easy now because I fish like this all the time. I can see from here. My eyes help me catch fish all the time. Just hang on tight both of you here we go."

Ernie dived quickly and picked up the cowboy by his loose fitting clothes and carried him over to Happy Happy Lake and dropped him in the lake. It happened so quiet and quick that the other cowboys did not know at first what to do. Then they quickly ran away.

When Ernie, Rudolph, and Anthony came back the train had started to move again but Ernie flew a little lower and the train engineer waved and hollered, "Thank you" to Ernie.

Ernie told Rudolph, "Your idea worked well. We really surprised those cowboys. I hope I did not hurt the cowboy. My claws are very strong. I tried to catch just his clothes to pick him up and carry him to the lake. He sure looked surprised when he was falling into the water. It will be something the cowboys and the train riders can talk about for a long time. It was fun too."

"It really was," said Rudolph "and thank you Ernie. I'm happy Anthony and I were with you to see you do this."

"Thank you," said Ernie.

Ernie, Rudolph, and Anthony flew around Nicely Nicely Winter Rest looking the place over a little more then Ernie landed where he first picked his friends up.

Rudolph and Anthony told Ernie thank you and Ernie said, "I'll go rest now too. This has been fun. See you both again later."

And Anthony and Rudolph agreed that was a nice ride. They also talked about how surprised that cowboy must have been to be picked up and dropped in Happy Happy Lake. Then they ate and rested at the Nicely Nice Open Hotel. They stayed close by for a few weeks having a good time because they were on vacation.

One morning after eating a good breakfast of bugs and most delicious flower nectar at the Open Hotel Restaurant, Anthony and Rudolph were just flying around when Anthony said, "Look Rudolph isn't that Hasty and Marie snail over there coming this way?"

Rudolph said, "Yes Anthony that does look like them. Let's go over and say hello."

When they got there it was Hasty and Marie. Rudolph and Anthony told them both hello and asked how they came. Hasty and Marie told them they came on the Rabbit Choo Choo and that it was a nice trip all the way, no trouble at all.

"We certainly had a nice ride. That's nice Anthony answered we came on the Rabbit Choo Choo too. Enjoy your visit this is a nice place."

Many of Rudolph and Anthony's friends kept coming to Nicely Nice Winter Rest. Rudolph and Anthony had been there for a long time and Rudolph told Anthony "It's time to go back to the Very Best Summer Place now. We better leave soon and tell our friends we are leaving. It's been nice here for the winter.

Hope you had a nice time Anthony."

"Oh yes it was very nice. Thank you for inviting me Rudolph."

About that time Rupert Bullfrog drove by in his car and said "Hi Rudolph and Anthony haven't seen you in awhile. How is everything?"

"Oh, we're ok," said Anthony and Rudolph "We're thinking of going back to Very Best Summer Place soon. We have been here for the winter. It's time to go back now."

"You know," said Rupert "I'm going back soon too. Would you like to ride back in my car? It's pretty big. It has two seats in back you could each have a seat.

"Anthony you could send your car back on the train? The road is pretty close to the Rabbit Choo Choo track. You could see your car most of the time."

"Think about it. If you want to ride with me we can leave anytime you want to go. I'm going for a swim at that little lake right over there. Think about it. Let me know, we could all ride back together."

Anthony and Rudolph thought about it, talked about it, and decided to ship Rudolph's little car back on the Rabbit Choo Choo and ride back with Rupert Bullfrog in his car. The three decided to leave together, so the next morning, right after the sun came up, they put everything in Rupert's big car. They packed their bags with some donuts, Anthony liked donuts, some sweet flower nectar for Rudolph and bugs for Rupert, Anthony also liked bugs with his donuts. They also packed their jackets. Rupert had a jacket made of yellow duck feathers and said he wanted to see the snow in Hoppity Mountains. He heard about the snow but never seen it before. Rupert always wore a cowboy hat when he drove his big car. Anthony asked Rupert if he had had his car checked and Rupert said he has filled it with sunshine for the trip back.

Rupert said, "Yes, everything's ok."

So everybody hopped in and zoomed away. They went in Rupert's big car with Rupert driving, Anthony in the middle seat and Rudolph in the back seat. On their way back to the Very Best Summer Rest from Nicely Nice Winter Rest, they planned to stop at the Happy, Happy Lake Resort to visit Flower Bug Island because Rupert Bullfrog had heard about the old buildings on Flower Bug Island and the Twilight Rainbow and the mermaids that come to watch it each evening.

With his heavy bullfrog voice and wearing his cowboy hat, Rupert said, "I have never seen a mermaid, I want to see a mermaid, I heard they're very beautiful." Rupert likes cowboy hats. Everything went nice. Rupert liked to drive fast. The road back was pretty close to the track the Rabbit Choo Choo traveled on.

Rupert reminded Anthony, "See Anthony we will be able to see your car on the train. The train left for Very Best Summer Rest not too long ago. We will probably see it pretty soon."

They had traveled not too far away when they saw the train. It was moving along pretty fast. Anthony and Rudolph could see their friend Bill Rabbit driving. He had his arm out the engine window and he could see his brother Jerry Rabbit sitting on the other side. They could also smell the carrot celery soup and other tasty food being cooked in the train kitchen. Anthony and Rudolph waved at Bill Rabbit and he waved back. Rupert Bullfrog waved too.

Rupert asked, "You know the driver?"

"Yes," Rudolph said "They are our friends. We know Bill and Jerry from Nicely Nice Summer Rest."

"Oh," said Rupert, "That's nice."

"That soup sure smelled good," said Anthony.

"Yes it did," said Rupert and Rudolph. "They have good cooks on the train."

Then the road came to a sharp turn. So did the railroad. The train stopped and the engine turned over,

and so did most of the cars. Rupert stopped right away, because the road was close to the railroad track at that place too.

When Rupert, Anthony, and Rudolph got there, they could see a large tree had fallen across the railroad track. Bill and Jerry did not see the tree in time to stop the train so the train hit the tree and turned over.

They could see Bill and Jerry, they seemed okay. They could hear Bill say very loudly to Jerry, "TURN OFF THE SUNSHINE. DON'T LOSE THE SUNSHINE."

"I did," said Jerry.

The kitchen car was almost to the back of the train near the Little Red Caboose and it did not turn over. Rudolph and Anthony were flying around together and Rudolph was watching near the engine. Anthony heard the cooks say, "cover the soup so it doesn't spill."

Then Rudolph said, "Look Anthony, that eagle that just landed looks like Ernie. Let's go see if that is Ernie." They both went over and spoke to Ernie. Ernie said he had gotten up early, was just flying around, saw the Rabbit Choo Choo, saw it turn over, and came to see if he could help.

Ernie said he had seen a few animals together not too far away. He would go ask them if maybe they wanted to help. "Do you want to go?" asked Ernie. Rudolph had already introduced Rupert the Bullfrog to Ernie. Ernie said "You three want to go? Hop on; I feel strong this morning. Hang on, here we go!"

Rupert said, "This is nice; I have never flown before. There are the animals in that big group over there."

"Some kind of meeting I think" said Ernie. "I'll land and we will tell them about the train wreck."

Ernie landed and told them about the train wreck. The animals all thanked Ernie, Alfred, Rudolph, and Rupert, and said they would go right over because the railroad was close by. There was Elley Elephant and his friend Bob Elephant that just happened to be visiting and had found the group of early morning risers for a meeting. Everyone came together and was happy for the nice weather with sunshine and a very nice spring season. Then they planned to go to Nicely Nice Winter Rest

Hotel Open Restaurant and vacation for a few days. But now they will hurry over and help with the train wreck. Ernie and his friends thanked everyone. Anthony, Rupert, and Rudolph climbed on and Ernie was up and away to the train wreck again. All the animals were on their way and soon arrived.

Elley and Bob Elephant looked at the engine, and said this will be easy. Bob said "I'll pick up this side of the engine and Elley you push."

Andy Alligator was there too and said, "I'll push too." Several other animals said, "we'll push on the cars." Everybody pushed and the train was back on the tracks real fast.

The engine windows and some of the car windows were dirty. Elley and Bob Elephant said, "We'll take care of that."

Ernie, who was watching too, said "I saw a little lake not far away where you can get water. I'll show you where it is. Hop on guys, you can go too!" Anthony, Rupert, and Rudolph hopped on. Away they went.

Ernie flew low calling out directions to Elley and Bob where the little lake was. They drank a lot of water, hurried back, and squirted it on the window. Hoppity Kangaroo hopped up with some grass in his hands and wiped off the window. Bill and Jerry turned on the sunshine and the cooks got the kitchen going.

Elley and Bob took the tree that fell down off the track. Bill, Jerry, and all of the passengers on the train thanked everybody and the Rabbit Choo Choo, blowing smoke, went right on down the track with cooks cooking delicious carrot celery soup.

Anthony, Rudolph, and Rupert thanked Ernie for all the help. Ernie told them you are very welcome and said, "I'll fly over now and then and check on you guys. I fly high and can see a long way too. It's easy and fun for me. See you!" and Ernie was up and away.

The animals all left too on their way to Nicely Nice Winter Rest Open Hotel Restaurant for a few days spring vacation. Everybody was happy and thanked each other for helping and glad that they were all there and able to help. Everybody felt good.

Rupert, Anthony, and Rudolph stopped at Happy Happy Lake Resort. The train had already gotten there for its three day stay. They saw Bill and Jerry the engineers again. Bill and Jerry thanked them again for helping and were happy everyone was there to help so quickly. Anthony, Rudolph, and Rupert said, "That's okay, that's what friends are for."

Then they found their friend Andy Alligator; he rode down with the train from the train wreck. He had went there for the spring meeting too, but was back to run his ferry service. He took Rupert, Anthony, and Rudolph over to Flower Bug Island because Rupert wanted to see the Twilight Rainbow and the mermaids he had heard about. He had heard they were very beautiful and he wanted to see for himself.

So when twilight came, Anthony and Rudolph made sure they rode the little train. Red, the Flower Bug Island train driver was driving and took them to where the Twilight Rainbow and mermaids could be seen. Rupert was very very happy and wore his cowboy hat all the time.

Then they left Flower Bug Island, thanked Andy Alligator for showing them the island. They said they would tell Ollie Crocodile they met him and that Andy said hello and thank you for sending his friends.

Soon they were back in Rupert's car on their way to Very Best Summer Place.

On the way, they stopped at Chilly Station and Rupert got to see the snow and wear his feather jacket made of yellow duck feathers. They got stuck in almost the same place Anthony did with his car and Jimminy Squirrel and Quickly Rat helped push them out. Anthony gave them some donuts and they were happy. They said they thought Rupert looked nice with his yellow feather jacket and cowboy hat. They had never seen a bullfrog in a nice jacket and hat like that before. Rupert told them thank you. They all said goodbye to their other friends that they had met in the great Hoppity Mountains. Then Rupert sped off in his big car.

They also stopped off in the little town the train passed through on their way to Nicely Nice Winter Rest and showed Rupert Deeply Creepy Cave and the fireflies lighting the lanterns, who had been tired and wanted to rest on the last trip. This time, Terry Turtle told the fireflies if they did not light up, he would tell Tom Beaver the manager and they might lose their jobs. The fireflies said, "okay, okay, okay Terry, we'll rest another time." But they kept mumbling very quietly to themselves that Terry was a grumpy old Turtle and that yeah, yeah, yeah he is.

Terry heard them and said, "Quiet in there you guys."

Then one firefly said, "see, I told you." Then the others said "sshhh sshhh shhh." But this time thelanterns did not go out like before when Anthony and Rudolph went through the cave. The fireflies worked all the way giving light. Everything else was the same in Deepy Creepy Cave.

When they came out Tom Beaver asked how they liked the cave. They told him that they had a nice time.

They were soon back in the car and on their way to the Very Best Summer Place. Then Rupert and Anthony told Rudolph "thank you for a nice vacation. We had a good time."

"You are welcome everybody," said Rudolph.

"You know I heard a story about a sailor in a ship wreck that was in a small boat and saw a little island with a wee small valley. He looked down in the valley and saw a little train with Rabbits driving it and smelled carrot celery soup. He later told others about it, but no one could ever find the place. They told him he must have been out on the water too long and was delirious and out of his mind. He said no, he had seen the place.

Anthony and Rudolph laughed and Rupert laughed too and they said the sailor was right; those folks just don't know. "Say, come to think of it, there was a ship wreck; we saw it on Flower Bug Island."

"Wasn't there" Anthony said.

"Sure was" Rudolph and Rupert said, "we both saw it."

Hey, if you're travelling near Nicely Nicely Summer Place and you see a wee small valley, see smoke and smell carrot celery soup, look close, you just might see the Rabbit Choo Choo passing through.

Bye Bye

Albert Vicent

Printed in the United States
By Bookmasters